Conversations with Peter Taylor

Literary Conversations Series
Peggy Whitman Prenshaw
General Editor

Photo by J. William Broadway

Conversations with Peter Taylor

Edited by Hubert H. McAlexander

University Press of Mississippi
Jackson and London

91   90   89   88   4   3   2   1

The paper in this book meets the guidelines for permanence and durability of the Committee on
Production Guidelines for Book Longevity of the Council on Library Resources.

Library of Congress Cataloging-in-Publication Data

Conversations with Peter Taylor.

  Includes index.
  1. Taylor, Peter Hillsman, 1917–   —Interviews.
2. Authors, American—20th century—Interviews.
I. Taylor, Peter Hillsman, 1917–   .   II. McAlexander,
Hubert Horton.
PS3539.A9633Z6   1987   813'.54   87-13679
ISBN 0-87805-324-7
ISBN 0-87805-325-5 (pbk.)

British Library Cataloguing in Publication data is available.

Books by Peter Taylor

A Long Fourth and Other Stories. New York: Harcourt, Brace, 1948.

A Woman of Means. New York: Harcourt, Brace, 1950.

The Widows of Thornton. New York: Harcourt, Brace, 1954.

Tennessee Day in St. Louis. New York: Random House, 1957.

Happy Families Are All Alike. New York: McDowell, Obolensky, 1959.

Miss Leonora When Last Seen and Fifteen Other Stories. New York: Ivan Obolensky, 1964.

The Collected Stories of Peter Taylor. New York: Farrar, Straus and Giroux, 1969.

Presences: Seven Dramatic Pieces. Boston: Houghton, Mifflin, 1973.

In the Miro District and Other Stories. New York: Knopf, 1977.

The Old Forest and Other Stories. New York, Dial, 1985.

A Stand in the Mountains. New York: Frederic C. Beil, 1985.

A Summons to Memphis. New York: Knopf, 1986.

Contents

Introduction

Peter Taylor, now seventy, has been a much acclaimed writer throughout his career of fifty years. The first of his many literary honors came in 1942, the year "The Fancy Woman" was chosen for the Best American Short Stories annual. When his *Collected Stories* appeared in 1969, Joyce Carol Oates hailed it as "one of the major works of our literature." Reviewing *The Old Forest and Other Stories* in 1985, Anne Tyler acknowledged Taylor as "the undisputed master of the short story form," and she placed herself in a generation of writers "who have practically memorized all he has produced." Among his intimates, Peter Taylor has been almost equally celebrated for his easy manner, his genuine affability, and his enthusiasm. *Conversations with Peter Taylor* offers the pleasure of encountering a distinguished literary figure who is also a warm and engaging personality.

This volume collects fourteen interviews (one previously unpublished) given between 1960, when "Venus, Cupid, Folly and Time" won the O. Henry First Prize, and 1987, shortly after Taylor published *A Summons to Memphis*. By 1960, of course, Taylor had been writing for twenty-three years. He was the author of three collections of short stories, a play, and a novel. Taylor stories had regularly appeared in both prestigious American Short Story annuals, and for over a decade he had contributed to the *New Yorker*. Unfortunately the few interviews published before 1960 are too slight to merit reprinting. The heading of one from a Columbus, Ohio, newspaper—"He 'Writes for Fun,' But His Stories Sell"—regrettably reflects the quality of the lot.

Had someone come forward with the right questions in those early years, the results would have been quite different, for even in those encounters there are glimpses of a man with a clear sense of himself and of his craft. In one strange piece in a 1950 Memphis newspaper (which evolves into an interview with Taylor's father about his son's work), Peter Taylor makes a particularly articulate statement about the importance of writing for him, and in addition he suggests the way in which his work should be approached:

> I began by writing about the scenes and the people I know best and much later began to discover what and who they were. I am still in the process of making that discovery and hope to remain so as long as I live. But in the end I don't mean what and who in a political or sociological sense. In my stories, politics and sociology are only incidental. I make the same use of them that I do of customs, manners, household furnishings, or anything else that is part of our culture. But the business of discovery of the real identity of the images that present themselves is the most important thing about writing fiction. Ultimately it is the discovery of what life is all about. As long as one writes, the process must go on. Until a writer learns something about the story he is writing or finds himself making observations he didn't know he was capable of, his story probably won't be any good. This is true, I suspect, for any writer, no matter how practiced, no matter what age.[1]

This view of his art has remained constant for Peter Taylor over the thirty-seven years since he made the statement.

But there has also been development, a maturing as a writer; and the interviews collected here reflect that process. We learn that Taylor was not long satisfied with writing Jamesian gems like "A Spinster's Tale." We discover his increasing concern with seeing for himself and presenting to the reader the multiple sides of characters, issues, and situations. We listen to his often detailed remarks about his allegorical stories, ghost plays, and verse-stories. The process of development leads in the last few years to the longer stories with reflective narrators and to his recent novel. As that path is traced, we learn of his increasing interest in plot; of his sometimes uneasy relationship with Henry James, the great mentor; of his reason for viewing "Miss Leonora When Last Seen" and "Venus, Cupid, Folly and Time" as milestones in his career. In a way, the cumulative effect of the interviews is similar to that of a late Peter Taylor work in which a mature man looks back over his life and muses on the pattern of development that he sees there. But we become aware of some

---

[1] Robert Richards, "Part of Memphis May Come Alive in Next Novel by Peter Taylor," Memphis *Press-Scimitar*, 22 October 1950, sec. 1, p. 18.

things that even Taylor himself did not realize at the time that he had some of these conversations. For example, we can discern the origins of his 1986 novel *A Summons to Memphis* as far back as the 1977 interview with Louise Davis—long before he was thinking of writing the novel. And we can follow the evolution of that work through the remaining encounters in the volume.

Of course we come to know not only the artist, but also the man—his liking for physical labor, his social curiosity, his need for social stimulation, his aesthetic sense. We listen as he reflects on the complex relationship between personality and history, on the importance of role in human life, and on the possibilities for both sustenance and entrapment offered by the social order. Throughout the collection, Taylor also provides us with a wealth of literary anecdote. We learn fascinating bits not only about Taylor himself, but also about the intersecting lives of other important writers of his time—John Crowe Ransom, Allen Tate, Caroline Gordon, Robert Lowell, Jean Stafford, and Randall Jarrell.

Peter Taylor occupies an unusual place in American literature, and the interviews cumulatively reveal the two sides of Taylor that make him the unique writer he is—that singular combination of Jamesian craftsman and southern storyteller. Along the way we hear some wonderful stories that have never made their way into the fiction.

The question of selection for a volume such as this one always presents problems. Although I was not confronted with the mass of material that has been the lot of some other editors in this series, still I had to make choices. Some of the interviews conducted in the last five years (the period during which most Taylor interviews were granted) are as slight as the very early ones. Others from this period, however, simply cover too much of the ground that is charted more thoroughly elsewhere. These too I omitted. In a collection of this sort some repetition is still inevitable. But readers should be wary when they are tempted to skip over matters that have been discussed before. For example, though Taylor talks about the writing of "Heads of Houses" several times, he offers two different readings of the story (see the Goodwin interview of 1973 and the Broadway exchange of 1985). Again and again, Taylor speaks in the highest terms of Randall Jarrell's interest in his friends' writing and his displeasure when he felt

they had fallen short of their best work. Thus in the interview with
Barbara Thompson, one is surprised and fascinated to find Taylor
voicing a different perception of Jarrell's response:

> He wanted me to have a very light touch, Chekhovian, not to have much
> serious event in it. I think he really thought of me as the Southern
> regional writer of memoir stories. He used to say, "Write all those stories
> you can, because that is a world that's gone, will never exist again, and
> this record of it should exist." So when I wrote that story, "Venus, Cupid,
> Folly and Time," he was very unsympathetic. Your friends often do this,
> when you want to change and are trying to do something else, and
> they've liked the other you. But you know, I never could go back and
> write those stories, the tone of which pretended to be just memoirs of
> genteel families.

The impact of the revelation is much stronger for our having heard
other versions of the matter.

In accordance with the policies of the Literary Conversations series,
the interviews are reprinted uncut. All ellipsis points are reproduced
from the original version. In some instances, the interviewer has gone
over the original printed version for me, correcting typographical
errors, supplying omitted words, etc. In the others, I have done that
job, which includes placing the titles of longer works in italics and
supplying missing punctuation marks. I have also found it advisable
to correct errors of fact (dates, for instance). These corrections are
made in brackets in the text.

The chronological order of publication in which the interviews are
presented here reflects the order in which they were given—except for
the final interview conducted by Barbara Thompson for *The Paris
Review*. Though it will not appear in that journal until shortly before
this volume is published, it is drawn from conversations beginning in
1981 and continuing through 1986. Because of the scope of the
interview, this extended conversation over five years supplements the
exchanges published earlier and serves as a fitting conclusion for this
collection.

Several interviews are prefaced by a sketch of Taylor's career. Thus
we are given some facts and presented with certain critical opinions of
Taylor's work more than once. One advantage of retaining this
material in the reprinted versions is that we are provided with a
running history of Taylor's career over the twenty-seven years. We are
also reminded at just what point in the career the particular interview

took place. In some cases, the background material given also explains the shape of the interview. The two interviews that appeared in Memphis publications offer an interesting example. There is a great difference between Taylor's good-humored attempt to answer the kinds of questions put to him in 1960 by Edwin Howard, who regards him as an emerging Memphis writer, and the way Taylor engages the questions in 1987 of W. Hampton Sides, who is fully aware of Taylor's importance in American literature.

My debts for this book begin in the English Department at the University of Georgia, and I wish to thank Coburn Freer, Walter Gordon, William Provost, and Michael Hendrick for various services and favors. Both Susan Tyler and Lee Jones aided me at different stages as part-time research assistants. My work in tracking down all the Taylor interviews was made much easier by Stuart Wright's willingness to exchange information. His Taylor bibliography will be published about the same time as this book. Barbara Rystrom and her staff in the Interlibrary Loan Department of the University of Georgia Library were most helpful in securing copies of some of the interviews for me. Thomas K. McCraw, Henry Hurt, Gina McNeal, Mary Eleanor Wyatt, Glenda Thompson Minion, Frances Nicol Teague, Katherine Baird Taylor, and Steven J. Ross all supplied information. Ronald Bogue and Patricia Jewell McAlexander offered valuable suggestions on the project. Finally, I am particularly grateful for the help, but even more for the graciousness, kindness, and warmth of Peter and Eleanor Ross Taylor.

HHM
February 1987

Chronology

1917   Peter Matthew Hillsman Taylor is born 8 January in Trenton, Tennessee, the fourth child of Matthew Hillsman Taylor and Katherine Baird (Taylor) Taylor.

1924   The family moves to Nashville.

1926   Hillsman Taylor accepts the presidency of the General American Life Insurance Company, and the family moves to St. Louis. There Peter Taylor attends Miss Rossman's School, 1926–29, and St. Louis Country Day School, 1929–32.

1932   The family settles in Memphis, and Peter Taylor is enrolled at Central High School.

1935   Taylor graduates from high school with a scholarship to Columbia University, where he intends to study writing. This plan is contrary to his father's desire that he enter Vanderbilt and prepare himself for a career in law. After graduation Taylor and a friend work their way to England on a freighter, and upon his return Taylor delays entering college.

1936   In the spring semester Taylor registers at Southwestern at Memphis. His freshman composition teacher is Allen Tate, who persuades him to go to Vanderbilt in the fall and study under John Crowe Ransom. At Vanderbilt, Taylor begins a lifelong friendship with Randall Jarrell.

1937   In March and April, Taylor publishes his first stories in *River,* a literary magazine in Oxford, Mississippi. Ransom leaves Vanderbilt for Kenyon College at the end of the spring term, and Taylor decides not to return to Vanderbilt. Instead he gets a job selling real estate in Memphis.

1938   Taylor enters Kenyon in the fall and forms a close friendship
       with Robert Lowell, who has also followed Ransom there.

1940   After graduation from Kenyon, Taylor and Lowell (now
       married to Jean Stafford) begin graduate study at Louisiana
       State University under Robert Penn Warren and Cleanth
       Brooks. Taylor, who has sold a poem to *Kenyon Review* and
       two stories to *Southern Review,* leaves the program at
       Thanksgiving.

1941   In June, Taylor is drafted. As a member of a company formed
       in Memphis, he is stationed for the next two and a half years
       at Fort Oglethorpe, near Chattanooga, Tennessee.

1942   "The Fancy Woman," first published in *Southern Review,* is
       selected for *The Best American Short Stories 1942,* edited by
       Martha Foley. This is the first of nine Taylor stories to appear
       in this annual between 1942 and 1980.

1943   In April, Allen Tate introduces Taylor to Eleanor Lilly Ross of
       Norwood, North Carolina. A graduate of Woman's College of
       North Carolina at Greensboro, she is then a student at
       Vanderbilt. After a courtship of six weeks, they are married on
       4 June at St. Andrew's School chapel near Sewanee, Ten-
       nessee, by Father James Harold Flye. In attendance are
       Robert Lowell and Jean Stafford, Allen Tate and Caroline
       Gordon.

1944   In February, Taylor's company is sent to Camp Tidworth in
       England.

1945   Taylor is discharged in December with the rank of sergeant.

1946   Allen Tate arranges a job for him at Henry Holt Publishers
       beginning in April, and the Taylors rent an apartment in
       Greenwich Village. In the fall Taylor takes a position in the
       English department at Woman's College of the University of
       North Carolina.

1947   The Taylors and the Randall Jarrells buy a duplex in Greens-
        boro. This is the first of nearly thirty houses that the Taylors
        will own.

1948   Taylor's first collection, *A Long Fourth and Other Stories,* is
        published in March with an introduction by Robert Penn
        Warren. In the fall Taylor goes to Indiana University as
        assistant professor and director of the creative writing pro-
        gram. Katherine Baird Taylor is born 30 September. Taylor
        begins a long association with the *New Yorker* when his story
        "Middle Age" is published there in November.

1949   He returns to Woman's College at Greensboro. *The Death of
        a Kinsman,* his first published play, appears in *Sewanee
        Review.*

1950   Taylor's novel *A Woman of Means* is published in May. He is
        awarded a Guggenheim Fellowship for 1950–51. "Their
        Losses" is selected for the O. Henry prize collection for 1950.
        This is the first of six Taylor stories to appear in the O. Henry
        annuals between 1950 and 1982.

1952   He is awarded a National Institute of Arts and Letters grant.
        For the spring term he is a visiting professor at the University
        of Chicago, and in the fall he goes to Kenyon College as
        associate professor in English and drama. Taylor serves as
        advisory editor for the *Kenyon Review* from 1953 to 1959.

1954   *The Widows of Thornton* (eight stories and a short play) is
        published in April.

1955   The Taylors' second child, Peter Ross Taylor, is born 7
        February. Taylor receives a Fulbright grant for 1955–56 to do
        research in Paris for a play about Southerners who settled
        there after the Civil War. Enroute to France, he lectures at the
        Fourth Conference on American Studies at Oxford University.

1956   The Taylors spend the summer at Rapello, Italy.

1957   Taylor's play *Tennessee Day in St. Louis* is published in
        February. It premieres at Kenyon in April. Taylor joins the
        faculty of Ohio State University to teach from January to
        June each year.

1958   The Taylors spend the summer in Bonassola, Italy (while the
        Randall Jarrells and the Robert Kitzgeralds are living at
        nearby Levanto), and the fall in Rome.

1959   "Venus, Cupid, Folly and Time" wins the O. Henry first
        prize. *Happy Families Are All Alike,* Taylor's third collection of
        stories, is published in November. It wins the Ohioana Book
        Award the next year.

1960   Eleanor Ross Taylor publishes *Wilderness of Ladies,* the first
        of her three volumes of poetry. The Taylors purchase a
        cottage at Monteagle, Tennessee, and establish their pattern
        of living there in the summers. Taylor spends the 1960–61
        school year in London studying at the Royal Court Theatre
        on a Ford Foundation Fellowship.

1961   Taylor's story "Reservations" is presented as "Delayed Honey-
        moon" on the U.S. Steel Hour in September.

1963   Taylor returns to the University of North Carolina at Greens-
        boro as Professor of English, teaching fiction writing.

1964   *Miss Leonara When Last Seen and Fifteen Other Stories*
        appears in February. In the fall Taylor serves as Visiting
        Professor at Harvard.

1965   Taylor's father dies in Memphis on 13 November. Taylor is
        awarded a Rockefeller Foundation grant to devote the 1966–
        67 school year to writing.

1967   Taylor's sister Sally Taylor Fitzhugh dies in Memphis in the
        spring. Taylor joins the English department at the University

of Virginia. With Robert Lowell and Robert Penn Warren, he edits the memorial volume *Randall Jarrell, 1914–1965*.

1968   His play *A Stand in the Mountains* is published in *Kenyon Review*.

1969   Taylor's mother dies on 18 May in Memphis. He is inducted into the National Institute of Arts and Letters on 21 May. *The Collected Stories of Peter Taylor* is published in August.

1970   "Two Images," the first of Taylor's "Ghost Plays," appears in *Shenandoah*.

1971   *A Stand in the Mountains* is first performed on 25 May at the Barter Theatre, Abingdon, Virginia.

1973   *Presences: Seven Dramatic Pieces* is published in February. Taylor serves as Visiting Professor at Harvard for the fall semester.

1974   In the summer Taylor has a heart attack at Clover Hill, his eighteenth-century residence outside Charlottesville. "The Instruction of a Mistress," the first of his verse-stories to be published, appears in the September issue of *The New Review*.

1975   Taylor is given a four-year appointment at Harvard. He resigns the appointment in June, and the Taylors buy a house in Key West and begin spending winters in Florida.

1977   *In the Miro District and Other Stories* is published in April. Taylor delivers the commemorative tribute to Robert Lowell at the American Academy and Institute of Arts and Letters in May.

1978   In May, the American Academy and Institute presents Taylor the Gold Medal for the Short Story.

1979   Taylor delivers the commemorative tribute to Jean Stafford at
        the American Academy and Institute in November.

1983   In May, Taylor is inducted into the American Academy of Arts
        and Letters; and in June, he retires from the University of
        Virginia.

1984   *A Woman of Means* is reprinted by Frederick C. Beil. The film
        version of Taylor's story "The Old Forest," produced and
        directed by Steven J. Ross of Memphis State University,
        premieres in Memphis in November.

1985   *The Old Forest and Other Stories* is published in February.

1986   *The Old Forest and Other Stories* wins the PEN/Faulkner
        Award for Fiction. *A Woman of Means* and the *Collected
        Stories* are reissued in paperback. Frederic C. Beil brings out
        a limited edition of Taylor's revised version of *A Stand in the
        Mountains.* Taylor suffers a stroke on 24 July. His novel *A
        Summons to Memphis* is published in October. Taylor with-
        draws the novel from the final list of three nominees for the
        American Book Award.

Conversations with Peter Taylor

Writer Peter Taylor Is Home

Edwin Howard/1960

From the Memphis *Press-Scimitar,* 25 March 1960, sec. 1, p. 7.

"No," the story begins, "Memphis in autumn has not the moss-hung oaks of Natchez. Nor, my dear young man, have we the exotic, the really exotic orange and yellow and rust foliage of the maples of Rye or Saratoga. When our five-month summer season burns itself out, the foliage is left a cheerless brown . . . and the air, the atmosphere (who would dare to breathe a deep breath!) is virtually a sea of dust. . . ."

The writer who knows Memphis so well and writes about it and other Southern locales so vividly—Peter Taylor—is back home in Memphis this week. The well-known author and teacher is visiting his parents, Mr. and Mrs. Hillsman Taylor, 5470 Poplar, and spending three days on-campus at Southwestern, which he attended in 1936 and '37, speaking to English classes and adult education groups.

The quotation above is from "The Walled Garden," which is included in Taylor's latest short story collection, *Happy Families Are All Alike,* published last November by McDowell, Obolensky.

Short story collections are usually prestige items, not expected to sell very well, but since the author has already collected from the magazines which originally published them, he is happy with a few sales and a number of complimentary reviews.

I thought I had detected a recent sales spurt for short story collections, though (Roald Dahl's *Kiss Kiss,* out less than a month, is already in ninth place on the United Press International list of fiction best-sellers and twelfth place on the *New York Times* list), so I asked Taylor how *Happy Families* was doing.

"It's doing better than anything else I've had published," he beamed. "In fact, it has already sold a good many more copies than my novel *(A Woman of Means)."*

How does a would-be author go about selling his stories? Must he have an agent? Dare he submit stories directly to the *New Yorker?*

3

"I've never had an agent," Taylor said. "Oh, I think I did have one briefly once, but I never will again. I used to work for one of the publishing houses in New York, and I know how their readers react to material submitted by an agent. Of course, if a writer turns out a tremendous volume of stuff or makes so much money he needs a business manager, he would probably want an agent."

How did Taylor sell his first story?

"I just submitted it. I didn't really sell my first one, though. They didn't pay anything. It was in a magazine called *River—Magazine of the Deep South.* It was published in Oxford, Mississippi, and Eudora Welty and several other Southern writers had some of their first stories in it."

But how did he make *New Yorker?*

"Actually, they wrote to me and asked me to submit some stories to them. They had read my stuff in some of the quarterlies. My first actual sale was to the *Southern Review,* published in Louisiana. That was [before] the war, about [1940]. Then I had stories in the *Sewanee Review* and the *Kenyon Review.*"

Taylor attended Southwestern two half-years, studying under poet Allen Tate (now teaching at University of Minnesota). Between times, he went to Vanderbilt and became a protege of John Crowe Ransom, whom he eventually followed to Kenyon College in Ohio, where he was graduated in 1940.

Now he's back at Kenyon, teaching courses in creative writing and drama. Some of his stories still appear in the *Kenyon Review;* one of them, "Venus, Cupid, Folly and Time," is included in *Best Short Stories of 1959,* just published by Ballentine.

Drama has long been a major interest of Taylor's, and he is about to make it a major pursuit, too. Later this year he will pack up with his wife, the former Eleanor Ross of North Carolina, and their two children, Katherine, 11, and Peter, 5, and head for London, where, under a Ford Foundation fellowship of $7500, he will "establish a close working relationship with the Royal Court Theatre."

What is a "close working relationship"?

"What it amounts to," Taylor explained with a grin, "is that they have to let me watch everything they do. I am just a neophyte in the theatre, but I would like to write for the theatre, so I'm to be allowed to sit in on all their productions for a year."

Although he considers himself a neophyte, Taylor has written several plays, and the Royal Court producers will read them and presumably offer suggestions and advice.

A full-length play Taylor wrote several years ago called *Tennessee Day in St. Louis* was given handsome, hardback publication in 1957 by Random House.

I was curious to know how he managed to get it published when at that time it had never been produced on Broadway or anywhere else. The Memphis author seemed to enjoy my curiosity, but could do little to satisfy it.

"I can't explain it myself," he said. "Of course, I had hoped they would want to publish it, but I had hoped it would be produced in New York, too. I would still love to see a Broadway production of it, and every now and then some producer or director will get all enthused over it. They'll call me long distance, and I'll think this is finally it. Then the whole thing is cold again."

Tennessee Day in St. Louis, the story of a family of displaced Southerners who celebrate "Tennessee Day" in their adopted St. Louis home, has been staged a few times outside New York now. Several colleges have performed it, a St. Louis television station did a production of it which Taylor missed, and a certain Little Theater did a production of it which he later wished he had missed.

"They made a big event of it," he recalled somewhat ruefully. "They had receptions and lots of publicity—and then they put on the play. It was one of the most excruciatingly painful experiences of my entire life. It was a terrible production. Finally, I was so embarrased that I just sneaked away into the night. They had another reception or cocktail party or something scheduled the second night, but I couldn't face it again."

An Interview with Peter Taylor

Stephen Goodwin/1973

From *Shenandoah,* 24 (Winter 1973), 3–20. Copyright © 1973 by Washington and Lee University, reprinted from *Shenandoah: The Washington and Lee University Review* with the permission of the editor.

Goodwin: Most of the people that you knew at Kenyon were poets. Did this have any effect on you?

Taylor: It had a very strong and lasting effect on me. Mr. Ransom was teaching at Kenyon while I was there, and so was Randall Jarrell, and my classmates, like Lowell, were almost exclusively interested in poetry. I think poets talked more about technical problems in those days, about meter and form, and they insisted upon closeness and structure and texture—those are words that they used a great deal—in writing. It's probably responsible for my turning into a short story writer rather than a novelist.

Goodwin: Did you write any poetry of your own?

Taylor: My ego required that I write poetry just to make an impression on that group. My interest in poetry had consisted of Whittier and such, which I had learned by heart as a boy, but at Kenyon I set about reading poetry of all kinds. At one point, Lowell and I decided that we were going to get out an anthology together and we went through centuries of poetry. And I wrote poetry for nearly the whole time I was there. The first thing I ever published, the first thing I was ever paid for, was a poem in the *Kenyon Review.* Mr. Ransom rather insisted on my writing poetry. I remember a piece I wrote for him, a story with a poem in it—you know how you want to get everything in when you're beginning to write. Well, Mr. Ransom read the story and returned it with a note at the top: *B* for the story, *A* for the poem. Mr. Ransom just wouldn't pay much attention to my fiction; Jarrell was the only one there who did. He was much more interested, even then, in characters in poetry than any of the others were. But even though Mr. Ransom condescended to fiction then—I think his attitude changed later, while he was editing the *Kenyon Review*—and insisted that I write poems, I learned a tremendous amount from him. When you're a young person working with a writer, I think that it's best for that time to try to learn what the writer can teach you. Mr. Ransom was a poet, so I wrote poems for him.

Goodwin: There must have been a good deal of competition in this group.

Taylor: I didn't feel that, and I don't think that I just won't admit it. We all wanted to publish, of course, but we weren't mad for publishing. I think we were more interested in each other's opinion than in the world's opinion. And in any literary clique people are going to have pretty much the same values; they're naturally going to like and admire each other's work if they're congenial, if they're all working on the same level. We did compete in other things, in grades—until I went to Kenyon I really didn't care about grades, but among Lowell and Jarrell and Macauley and John Thompson and all those people, I wanted to be good at what they were good at. I felt, for the first time, that I had found my peers.

Goodwin: Why did you turn back to fiction?

Taylor: I had always been interested in stories. In my family the Southern oral tradition really did persist; my family told stories constantly and talked about the past. But what I most wanted to be, like so many fiction writers, was a painter. My only serious early training was as a painter. I took classes in school and after school. When I went to Kenyon I was still painting; that was my real impulse.

Goodwin: Did any particular writers or books have a strong effect on you when you were growing up?

Taylor: I was terribly stirred by the first novel I read which touched on the kind of life I had seen. It was a book called *Within This Present* by Margaret Ayer Barnes, and I read it simply because it was in our house. The book was about Chicago, about people somewhat like my own family, and it just electrified me that you could write stories about them. I went on to read all of her books. She may not be a literary influence exactly, but I think that people often do get into writing in that way. After all, Chekhov wrote joke books first.

Goodwin: Did you know any writers before you went to Kenyon?

Taylor: I was lucky in growing up in Tennessee when I did. There were writers of the first rank around, men like Tate and Lytle and

Davidson and Ransom. They had almost the same background that I did, they were accessible to me—Lytle and my father were devoted friends—and I never felt the alienation from my background that some writers seem to feel. I never felt that the people at home were queer ducks, that I would have to go off somewhere in order to become a writer. Southern writers have generally stayed close to home, and though this may sound egotistical, I feel identified with Tennessee, North Carolina, and the upper South. I feel that it's a part of me and that I'm a part of it. Other Southerners seem to feel this as strongly as I do. I once found myself at a conference of Southern writers out in North Dakota, along with two mountaineer novelists and a man from the Deep South and a Negro sculptor from Knoxville. We were questioned and heckled in public about being Southern, about identifying ourselves as Southern, but we all insisted that it was important to us. We stuck together absolutely. At night, back at the motel, we fought like cats and dogs about what it meant to be a Southerner, to be an artist, but in public we agreed entirely.

Goodwin: What about Faulkner? Flannery O'Connor once said that all Southern writers have to deal with Faulkner, that to write about the South without knowing your Faulkner was like having your mule and wagon stalled on the track with the Dixie Limited bearing down on you. Do you think of Faulkner as an obstacle or as a source?

Taylor: I think that we all ought to get down on our knees every night and thank God for Faulkner. He is the master; he taught us all to observe our own world, the benefits of observing it closely. Some writers make breakthroughs, and all writing has a great surge after that; everybody benefits from it. What gets borrowed or stolen doesn't matter, because a good writer always adds something, makes his particular mark. I'm not at all ashamed when somebody accuses me of stealing. I have stolen unconsciously, and I admit it. If you love a Chekhov or a Katherine Anne Porter or a Faulkner story so much, you can't help wanting to do something like it. You often will do something like it and more, and why worry about it? If the thief goes farther or in a different direction, what could be a greater compliment to the writer he stole from?

I don't think Eudora Welty could have written without Faulkner; by the same token, Eudora Welty made it possible for Flannery O'Connor to write. I think Flannery found things in certain stories of Eudora's, stories like "The Petrified Man" and "Keela, the Outcast Indian Maiden," that she could take and make her own. This is not to say that she imitated Eudora, any more than Eudora imitated Faulkner, but that Eudora introduced the kinds of subjects in her fiction, and handled them with a kind of comic sensibility that created a field for Flannery.

Goodwin: What writers other than Southern writers do you look to as your masters?

Taylor: Chekhov, of course, and Turgenev; I read all of Turgenev and really felt closer to him than to Chekhov. And Joyce, Frank O'Connor, D. H. Lawrence. I read Henry James and Proust and Thomas Mann. As a matter of fact, I always thought I had been influenced by Mann, and I wrote several stories that I believed were very much in the manner of Mann. Nobody else ever noticed it. "Skyline" is one of my Mann stories which is so far undetected. And it certainly doesn't seem like Mann to me, nowadays.

Goodwin: How do you actually, physically, do your writing?

Taylor: I don't use any outlines or notes. I just begin with the first sentence, first paragraph, and by the time I have a page or two—and that may take some while, at any rate—the margins are just crawling with things I've jotted down. What happens later in the story—the incidents, characterization, lines of dialogue—often comes from these messages I've written myself at the beginning. I don't mean to say that the whole story reveals itself in that first burst of energy, in those first pages. I wish it did. I usually have to wait for a second inspiration before I know how a story will end. The story may have taken a direction I hadn't foreseen, or I may have gotten interested in a different aspect of it, or the original may simply go bad—all sorts of things can divert that first impulse.

Goodwin: Do you then revise the first portion of the story?

Taylor: Not unless I have to. I try to hedge my bets. Of course I have to revise sometimes, and sometimes I've had to throw out an entire story. I had to dump a complete draft of "Heads of Houses" into the wastebasket.

Goodwin: Why?

Taylor: In the first version, I wrote the story out just as I had heard it. It was a story someone had told me, an anecdote, and I didn't have to change a detail. It was all there: a college professor and his wife visiting the wife's parents for the summer, all of them getting on each other's nerves so badly that the professor sends himself a fake telegram calling him back to school early. The wife's parents accept this; the professor loads up the car; but as he and his wife drive off, they turn for one last look and see the wife's parents and her brother, the three of them with their hands joined, dancing for joy in front of the house.

The trouble was that the story was still an anecdote, a joke. I hadn't made it a story. And I had found, in the writing, that the brother was the character who really interested me. The others were duller; they had their own lives and they were committed to them; but the brother saw more, observed more, knew more. He was the one I wanted to concentrate on. I had to focus on him to get at the meanings the story seemed to contain. And I finally had to give up what I liked most about the story, the ending, the three of them dancing in a circle. It was too corny, too silly. It simple wouldn't do, even though I started the story for the sake of that ending. It cost me something, but I gave it up. I think this must be one of the hardest things to do, for me and probably for other writers—to abandon something that you like enormously.

Goodwin: Are many of your stories based on stories that you heard at home or elsewhere? On characters that you knew?

Taylor: There was a period when I tried to see if I could make every speech in the dialogue in a story one that I had heard somewhere. And in some stories—like "Their Losses"—practically every word in even the smallest speech is one that I heard. And "A Spinster's Tale" is right out of my mother's mouth. My mother was rather prim and puritanical—'old-maidish,' we used to say, at least she had that side of her—and that story is really hers. Her mother died when she was fourteen, and she was right there in the house; there was a baby that died; the dreams in the story are her dreams, and there was a real Mr. Speed. The language in the story was my mother's too—it's more Victorian, more elevated than the language in most of my stories.

Lowell always teased me about that story. We were still at Kenyon when I wrote it, and he told me that *I* was prim and puritanical, that I didn't know anything about the world, that there wasn't enough of the roughness of life in my stories. So I vowed I'd show him, and I sat down and wrote the first sentence of "The Fancy Woman": *He wanted no more of her drunken palaver.* I had no idea where I was going from there, and then suddenly a whole story based on someone I knew, a father with two boys, just came to me. The story took over—well, it wasn't quite as simple-minded as that.

Goodwin: Faulkner spoke of the difficulty of a writer's ever knowing how much he drew from experience, how much from observation, how much from imagination. He said that even if he'd wanted to render a character faithfully, he would have ended up inventing him.

Taylor: Precisely. A writer uses his models just as a painter might use a model who's come in to pose for him. Suppose he happens to be painting the Agony or the Nativity—he doesn't have to have Jesus and Mary in the studio with him. He uses a model, a real man or woman, but he's not interested in an exact likeness. He distorts, composes, invents what he needs for the sake of the picture. Extreme examples might be El Greco or Modigliani. A writer treats his models in the same way. He turns them into characters. By the time a story is completed, that real person has been transformed into something quite different.

Goodwin: Doesn't dialogue too have to be tampered with? While Dos Passos was working on *U.S.A.,* he recorded hundreds of conversations with soldiers, but no one believed that the verbatim transcripts were authentic. They thought Dos Passos had cooked them up.

Taylor: And the opposite is true of Hemingway. No one ever talked the way people do in Hemingway, or at least I never met any one who did, and yet within the context of the story, the conversations seem perfectly acceptable and real. The reason I could use dialogue word for word in those stories of mine, stories like "Their Losses" or "Two Pilgrims," is that those stories were old stories, stories which had been told over and over again. Those speeches stayed the same time after time, and you know that when a story like that doesn't change, there must be something in it. By the time those stories came down to me, those speeches had been refined so that they revealed a great deal about the people who spoke them. So I didn't have to change a word.

Goodwin: Are any of your stories invented from whole cloth?

Taylor: I've worked some stories out just the way you'd work out a theorem. I spent months on "Venus, Cupid, Folly and Time," working out the theme of it, although I suppose I could probably mention somebody as the original of every character in that story. "Miss Leonora When Last Seen" is another story that I constructed just as deliberately as I could. Those two, "Venus, Cupid, Folly and Time" and "Miss Leonora," are for me complete allegories, although they may not be for the rest of the world. I don't think that matters very much. I was shocked to read what "The Dead" was supposed to mean to Joyce—and once you know all the secrets, your reading of the story is never the same, you're no longer innocent. Joyce may have required all that scaffolding, but that's not what makes the story a great story for the reader.

Goodwin: Are there any stories of yours which contain secrets, hidden meanings that you'd like to disclose?

Taylor: I did once write a story called "Reservations" which is just as sexy as I could make it. In a spirit of fun, I invented all sorts of Freudian symbols and phallic symbols—and they're appropriate to the story, too—but I wanted the story to be acceptable to what James always called the Dear General Reader, and my symbols are completely buried in the story. "Reservations" is just loaded with things that were unprintable in those days, with ungenteel suggestions. Well, the editors of *The New Yorker* apparently didn't see the story as I did and they printed it, and then it was translated and printed in a French ladies' magazine, with page after page of illustration, and finally it was made into a play by the United States Steel Hour. By this time I felt rather low, and I began to imagine that perhaps I had sold out, that I might only have imagined that it was a sexy story, and then I got a lovely letter from Randall Jarrell analyzing the story in the greatest detail and having caught every possible suggestion in it.

Goodwin: You and Jarrell taught together at Greensboro for several years. Did he have any influence on your stories?

Taylor: A great deal. I learned a lot about fiction from Randall. During those years he read my stories and made many suggestions, many of which I followed. He was very sympathetic, as people might not have suspected, to the Southern quality of my stories. He urged me to write about the South, to record it. He used to say, "This is all

going to be gone in a few years. It has to be written down now.
You're writing not just for literature but for posterity." He wanted a
very naturalistic tone in the stories—he objected to my more severe
stories, the more schematic stories like "Venus, Cupid, Folly and
Time," although he later came around to thinking it was one of my
best.

Goodwin: Have there been any special difficulties for you as a
Southerner to write about racial problems?

Taylor: I don't think I've ever written about racial problems. I've
always written about people who belong to a time and place that I
know. That place happens to be the upper South, and there are
people of different colors in it. There were Negro servants in the
house where I grew up; they were intelligent people and they showed
me a kind of affection—well, a kind of affection that white people
often find difficult to show. All I can do as a writer is write about them
as I knew them, try to understand them as I try to understand any
character. It may be that a writer's most important possession, after
his talent, is his sense of belonging to a time and place, whatever the
disadvantages or injustices or cruelties of that time and place may be.
The writer isn't going to change the world, or at least I'm not; I've
had to write about the world as I found it.

Goodwin: Let me ask you another question about "Reservations," or rather about sex in fiction. All sorts of new freedoms seem
to be available to the writer these days. Do you think your own
stories might have been different if they'd been written in a climate
like that which exists today?

Taylor: I don't think I would have written them any differently. I'm
writing things now in which the material is perhaps even more carnal
than in any of the stories, but I'm not interested in reproducing sex
scenes for the sake of titillating the reader. Randall Jarrell used to say
that 90% of the bedroom scenes and sex scenes in novels were
unnecessary, and I agree. I object to the full, prolonged descriptions
of sexual intercourse, the play-by-play accounts. To me, it's almost as
if the writer had described a marvelous dinner: he raised the glass of
wine to his lips, the rich liquid soothed his taste buds, he swallowed
and it went on down his gullet. To try to reproduce that, those
sensations, is not the business of fiction. The writer may want to
make the experience real and vivid for the reader, but often experi-

ence is much more real when suggested than when explicitly described. When sex becomes explicit, the writer loses the full
participation of the reader, drives him to voyeurism and peepholing
What the writer is interested in finally is the meaning of the experience, what the experience means to the characters, and he should
include only what he needs to convey that meaning.

It's not the job of the government or of committees to decide what's
permissible and what isn't. What can be written is a matter of what
custom allows and what readers find acceptable. There have been
sex scenes in novels for a long time; the new freedom is really a
freedom of language. You can now use language in fiction that you
couldn't use before. You can describe scenes in a way that you
couldn't a few years ago, and I suppose that if we all begin to talk like
certain characters in modern fiction, then all fiction will use that sort
of language. I think that nearly all good writers have been able to get
away with whatever they needed to get away with, that their work
always justified the language they had to use, that they've always
been able to present whatever the story required.

Goodwin: You said that you were a reader of Lawrence. What do
you think of his handling of sex?

Taylor: I remember reading *Lady Chatterly's Lover* when it first
came out. The bad words had all been left out. It was very exciting.
His *blank* and her *blank*. There's real suggestion for you. But I don't
think that that book, for all the time they spend in bed, has as much
genuine, intense sexuality as some of the other novels and the stories
where the sex is much more implicit. Of course, Lawrence at his best,
in his really great stories like "The White Stocking" and "The Horse-
Dealer's Daughter," is very much more than a sex writer. He's one of
the real masters of the short story. I've always thought so, and I've
always been puzzled by people who wonder how I can like Lawrence
and Joyce or Lawrence and Chekhov at the same time. Why
shouldn't I? Lawrence and Joyce are both masters, even if they are
poles apart. When you're reading one, you accept the truth of his
view; when you read the other, you accept his truth. It's absurd to
think that one somehow cancels out the other.

Goodwin: Lawrence, and Joyce too for that matter, are usually
thought of as novelists. Do you think that their stories have been

neglected? Do you think that the short story in general has been neglected?

Taylor: I can't help feeling that, but I wonder, if I were a novelist, if I wouldn't feel that short story writers were taken too seriously. The short story is supposed to be the American form, everyone says that Americans excel in it, and yet it's not nearly as popular as the novel. Stories just don't get you the glory or the fame, or the readers either. The only American magazine that really put the story forward, that seemed to consider the story a legitimate and serious form in its own right, was *Story* magazine, and it no longer exists.

Goodwin: What about *The New Yorker?* Many of your stories have been published there.

Taylor: There was a period shortly after the Second World War when *The New Yorker* attracted a number of literary people for the first time. The old-line *New Yorker* writers were mostly humorists, like Dorothy Parker or S. J. Perelman. After the war, they began to print Mary McCarthy and J. F. Powers and Jean Stafford and Eudora Welty and others who were among the best writers in the country. *The New Yorker* didn't discover them; they were already acknowledged as first-rate writers. They printed my stories too, but I always had the feeling that they were more interested in the subject matter than in the literary quality of the story. Ross, the editor, seemed to want certain kinds of pieces—period pieces, pieces concerned with regional differences. My stories were attempts to represent life in the cities and towns of the upper South, and I think he took them for the same reason that he took the Jewish stories and the Catholic stories. *The New Yorker* has changed now; it's more politically oriented than it used to be. That kind of bias, even though it may be very subtle, places as many restrictions on writing as the slick commercial magazines did.

It was always a pleasure to have *The New Yorker* edit a piece, to know that somebody with an absolutely literal mind would comb your story. The little magazines sometimes show too much respect. They won't catch you up in little inconsistencies. I once got from *The New Yorker* a full page discussion about the use of light switches in a story I had sent them. But the myth that *The New Yorker* changes stories to make them fit the tone of the magazine is just a myth; they never changed anything of mine. They did once object to the title of a story of mine. They didn't like the title "Je Suis Perdu." I don't know why. Because it was French? Anyway, I changed it to "A Pair of Bright Blue Eyes" and they printed it, and then I changed it back when it was collected in a book. "Je Suis Perdu" is obviously a better title.

Goodwin: Which of your stories are your own favorites?

Taylor: I like different stories for different reasons. I think that "Venus, Cupid, Folly and Time" and "Miss Leonora" are among the best stories I've written, but that may be because I worked so hard on them. I worked them out systematically, I assembled characters and situations to make them work as stories, I knew exactly what I was saying. After all the time I put in—I spent months and months on "Venus, Cupid, Folly and Time"—I feel I have to like those stories. And then I like other stories which came very easily, almost like memoirs, because they seem so natural as stories. "A Spinster's Tale" may be one of my best, but I hate to admit it; it was written right at the beginning, and no one likes to think he hasn't gotten better. "Je Suis Perdu" is one of my favorites, and that story just happened that way. Katie, my daughter, was the little girl who got lost in a movie theatre in Paris. When she called out to me, I didn't recognize her voice because she was calling in French. She was calling, "Je suis perdue," and I didn't really pay attention to her—I didn't know any French children. That story was one of Randall's favorites too. He even noticed that in the story the little girl uses the feminine *perdue,* with an *e,* but in the title the word is masculine, because it's the father who's lost.

Goodwin: Can you say why you've concentrated so on the short story, why you've written only one short novel?

Taylor: It may all go back to my training with Mr. Ransom. I still feel that everything in a work of art must be functional, must contribute, must be working. I'm bored by novels that do less with a chapter than a short story does with a sentence. In fact, I have to confess that I find most novels tedious. More than half of the contemporary novels that I read could have been done more effec- tively as stories. I really don't like to read any novels except great novels, novels that absolutely have to be novels. It may sound silly, but I believe that a long narrative, a novel, has to do as much more than a short story as an epic poem does than a lyric poem.

Goodwin: Did your own novel, *A Woman of Means*, present itself to you as a novel? Or did it begin as a story?

Taylor: That was a long manuscript. I actually cut it way down before it was published. It could have been much longer—but with nearly everything I've written, I've thrown away as much as I finally kept. And then there was some question about whether or not the publisher would publish it as a novel. The publisher sent me a great sheaf of letters explaining why it wasn't a good novel, and I answered by threatening to withdraw it, and the publisher wrote back saying he had decided to print it. Perhaps he still didn't like it but thought that I had other novels up my sleeve. Well, I do have one now.

Goodwin: What is it about? and how do you know it's a novel?

Taylor: Instead of one protagonist, I have three in this novel. They are three first cousins born in the same month of the same year. Their mothers are sisters, and they've had very much the same experience in life. There's a difference of temperament, of course, and the life they have lived has hit them in different ways. It's a problem that has always fascinated me: you can't help wondering at times, if you'd been made just a little bit differently, and if life had treated you somewhat differently, you might have ended up this person or that person. To fully understand the circumstances of any one life, what that life has become, you have to know what it might have been. I'm using the point of view of only one of the characters in writing the novel—I tried using all three but finally decided on one—but this one character is able to understand the others.

I felt that this idea required a novel. I think it requires a great deal of space and a great deal of time to appreciate what might have been. This story has to represent whole lives instead of suggesting just one kind of experience, a part of a life. I feel that lives of these characters must be known in detail, not just suggested.

Goodwin: Have you worked this novel out systematically, the way you worked out "Venus, Cupid, Folly and Time"?

Taylor: Not at all. These protagonists, the three cousins, are actually the sons, or grandsons, of the principal characters in a novel I was trying to write a few years ago. That novel finally became a play—it seemed to cry out to be a play. It was a piece of action that all took place in a certain time. I got rid of all the original major characters in the play, which I've more or less finished.

Goodwin: You've written several plays recently. Are you more interested now in drama than in narrative fiction?

Taylor: I'm much more interested in drama, or I will be if I can finish my novel and make a good job of it. I've always felt that the short story is a dramatic form and that it's much more natural for a short story writer to write plays than it is for him to write novels. There are plenty of examples of this: look at Chekhov and Pirandello and the Irish short story writers. Publishers harass short story writers for years, trying to get novels out of them, when a story writer's talent is much more apt to be for plays.

Goodwin: What for you is the difference between a story and a play?

Taylor: Certain subjects are more suited to plays. Some of my plays—"The Death of a Kinsman" is one—were written first as stories and later rewritten as plays, for that reason. There are themes and experiences that fiction simply can't handle convincingly. Or probably I should say, that this writer's fiction can't. That is, sometimes it becomes just too difficult for the novelist or short story writer not to be explicit and literal about the meaning of certain experiences and the psychology of certain characters. He has an awful choice. Either he explains when he shouldn't, or, for the sake of drama, he withholds vital information or vital knowledge until the end of the narrative. I find this latter extremely irritating. But either way, the author comes between us and what the story is trying to say. In a play, because of the blessed limitations of the form, it is at least not so obvious when information is withheld. And unless he is willing to descend to the coy device of a "narrator," the playwright cannot step in and explain. . . . Let me try to be still more specific. Ghosts and fantasies, I think, are a part of the experience of most people. Yet somehow or other, narrative seems always to get in the way of any serious writer's efforts to present ghosts and fantasies. Too many tricks are necessary. Furthermore, to consider the other side of the coin, I personally like ghosts, ghosts of the dead and ghosts of the living, because I know they tell me things about myself that I could not otherwise know. Several of my plays are ghost plays, plays in which a ghost makes an appearance to one or more of the characters. I believe an audience in a theatre, or even the readers of plays, are much more likely to accept this than readers of fiction are. I maintain that when Hamlet's father walks onto the stage, you don't question its reality. He's there. My experience with my own plays is just that: when a ghost enters the stage, you know he's a ghost, and there he is. To have a ghost in a story—and this is just practical— you've really got to work something up, which usually means that you've got to be very artificial. I'd consider a third side of the coin— an odd coin, I'll admit—the use of ghosts is a way of externalizing experience that could not otherwise be presented in a play.

Goodwin: It must be very seductive for a writer to see his story materialize before his eyes.

Taylor: The greatest joy is doing something with *people* after all the years of doing things off by yourself, and of course it's fun to see the plays done the way you want them done. I've had the good luck of having several plays produced at Kenyon, and the director there, James Michael—well, naturally, I think he's one of the best directors I've seen. He's been very faithful to my intention in the plays. He's tried to understand completely every play of mine that he's done, and then tried to make it answer my conception in every literal detail. And to see a play produced is more than just looking back over a story—it's almost like writing it again to see it done. But when a play is done badly, nothing could be more excruciating or painful than to have to sit through it. I've actually left town because I couldn't stand one more performance of a play of mine.

Goodwin: You've taught for a good many years, at Indiana, at Greensboro, and now at Charlottesville. Do you think that teaching is likely to be dangerous to a writer? That it's likely to keep him from his work?

Taylor: For years I've listened to the genuine sorrows of writers, writers who were also teachers. Teaching may be just deadly for a writer—as any other job may be—if you have a heavy academic load or hundreds of small bureaucratic duties. And there are some ways of thinking and talking about books that don't seem to help writers, or at least they don't help me. To discuss the ideas of Gide or Malraux or any other writer takes it out of you. I vowed I would never write another line of criticism after doing a review of Allen Tate's novel, *The Fathers,* and my record is clean. On the other hand, if you're teaching writing, if you're talking to writing students, people who are begin- ning to have their first insights, their first conceptions of fiction, and if you're talking about craft—that can be tremendously exciting. It's a joy to go to class and talk to people about stories, about their own stories—it's much more human than having numbers of individuals writing away privately and then sending their work out to be printed somewhere.

Goodwin: What do you think a writing teacher ought to try to do for his students?

Taylor: One is obligated to introduce students to great writers, to great writing. When I first began teaching, I had my classes read the *Kenyon Review, Sewanee, Partisan,* and other current fiction, until I realized that they hadn't read any stories before and really had no perspective on the story. I've come to the point now where I believe that if they're going to read contemporary stories, they'll do it on their own. They don't have to have it taught to them. I have my classes read Chekhov, Lawrence, the masters. I think they stand up pretty well. After all, people writing poetry still read the 17th century poets, don't they? They don't confine their reading to the little magazines. I feel very strongly that if you're introducing people to fiction, you've got to present them with more than what's *au courant,* what's going now. This works out very nicely for the teacher too; Jarrell and I exchanged secrets long ago. If he happened to be interested in a particular poet, you'd find that his classes were reading a lot of that poet. If I'm reading a lot of Faulkner or Lawrence, you'll usually see my students reading Faulkner and Lawrence.

Goodwin: What direction do you think your work will take in the future?

Taylor: I want to finish the novel that I'm working on, but I would like to spend most of my time writing plays. I'd like to have the plays produced, but I'm also terribly interested in having them read. I care very much about the language in them, and I often try to imagine myself as a reader when I'm writing them. People just don't seem interested in reading plays, either before seeing them or after— perhaps it's because the plays are so bad. But so many people tell me that they hate to read plays, it's always a glorious moment when someone says, "I love to read plays." I love those people. I try to write for them. I try to make each line work, make it interesting and revealing, just as I would in a story. One of the first rules of dialogue is that a line has to do more than just give information; it has to suggest the sound of the voice, has to be a characteristic speech. You can't just write, "Aunt Mary is arriving from Nashville on the 9 o'clock plane tomorrow morning"—in fiction you'd never allow yourself to do that.

Goodwin: Are you going to abandon stories?

Taylor: I doubt that I'll write many more short stories. I feel that I've done what I want to do as a short story writer. For years I was so absorbed in stories that I didn't think I would ever try to do anything else, but when I start a story now, I know that I can write it. Once you've learned how to do something as well as you can, you just don't care about repeating it. I don't mean to sound conceited, and I don't even mean that I'm satisfied with the stories; but I have a horror of repeating myself, of imitating myself. Some of my favorite writers have done that—Frank O'Connor, for example. He's a marvelous story writer, but after a point he was simply imitating his early stories. It's very difficult to see why the late stories aren't as good as the earlier ones, but they're not. And, as someone said, the story is the young man's form. After *Dubliners,* Joyce didn't want to write any more stories; Katherine Anne Porter, when she had written her stories, went on to other things.

Goodwin: What are your ambitions for your writing? How would you like people to think of it?

Taylor: I've never felt the way many writers do about being professional. My writing is a by-product of my efforts to understand my life; that's what it comes to. I'm always unhappy when I hear someone say, I don't think so-and-so's a very good writer, I've never read anything of his that I like, but he's real professional. I'd much rather have someone say about me, he's not professional, but he wrote a few things that were really inspired.

Just Who Was That Ward-Belmont Girl Nude in the Closet?

Louise Davis/1977

From *The Tennessean* [Nashville, TN], 20 February 1977, sec. E, 1, 4. Reprinted by permission.

Big guessing game around town since *The New Yorker*, in its Feb. 7 issue, published the latest of Peter Taylor's short stories about Nashville is: Who *was* that Ward-Belmont girl caught hiding without a scrap of clothes on in Grandfather Manley's wardrobe?

Taylor, distinguished short story writer who formerly lived in Nashville and is a grandson of Tennessee's noted Gov. Bob Taylor, smiles tolerantly at the guessing that follows each of his stories about Nashville or Memphis, or Monteagle or Beersheba Springs, for that matter.

And this week, in Key West, Fla., where he and his wife, Eleanor, were working alongside carpenters at their newest project—restoring an old home they recently bought—Taylor put the tools down long enough to discuss, by telephone, some of his writing secrets.

For one thing, being the gentleman he is, Taylor never tells tales and names too. Only the tales.

"I put Memphis people in Nashville, and Nashville people in Memphis," he said. "Or sometimes I get all of those names and people from North Carolina.

"I mix 'em up so people can't identify them. There's no use in making people mad."

But in this latest of his many stories published in *The New Yorker* (this one called "In the Miro District"), Taylor did give the leading character, the grandfather, the name of one of Taylor's own great-grandfathers, Basil Manley.

"Basil Manley [Taylor] was the name of my [father's] grandfather," Taylor said, "and he did have some of the same adventures in the

22

Civil War, and at Reelfoot Lake, where he was kidnapped by the night riders, as the character in the short story had."

Taylor said he felt safe enough in using that name, since he did not think there could be anyone alive today who would remember his ancestor.

"But I did hear from a lady in North Carolina who remembered him," Taylor said.

Sometimes readers are irate, Taylor said, because they think their city has been slighted, or they think they recognize someone in the story who is not wholly admirable.

So far, he has received only one letter from a Nashvillian since this latest story appeared, Taylor said. The story, evoking a whole era of Nashville in transit between country and city, revolves around a college boy's adventures at his parents' substantial home near West End Avenue, in Acklen Park.

"The man who wrote that letter wanted to discuss every detail of the story," Taylor said. "I expect I will get more, but the mail is slow."

Other readers over the nation may read Taylor's richly evocative stories of life in Nashville in the 1920s and 1930s for the easy-flowing narrative, the subtle interplay of characters, the hilarious scenes, the ironies, the quaint southern customs and "proprieties," the relentless impact of time and place on the people caught there.

But Nashvillians have a box seat on the action. They titter and gasp at the goings-on in the staid old homes that used to stand on West End Avenue, or Elliston Place, or on the Vanderbilt campus.

In other Nashville stories, when Taylor writes about romantic meetings at Candyland on West End, or at the Japanese Garden in Centennial Park, Nashville readers all but walk beside him. For part of Taylor's skill is to call up out of the past the mood of the moment, the street, the very room.

The truth of his ideas is undeniable, and so are his characters. But he shuffles them around in various disguises, sometimes combining two people into one. He may combine two grandfathers into one, for instance, as he did in this latest story about Nashville. But always the dilemma of the grandfather runs true.

"I showed a country grandfather who went down in defeat against city mores," Taylor said in an interview. "Actually my real grandfather never did give in—the one who was model for my story. But the other grandfather did. I used the two to create a more complex character."

Part of Taylor's consideration for privacy is to disguise the name of small towns or country communities he writes about. In this latest story, "In the Miro District," for instance, he has the sturdy grandfather driving in to Nashville from his farm 40 miles away in a fictitious county he calls "Hunt County."

But Taylor's own grandfather [Taylor] came from Trenton, in Gibson County, where Taylor was born in 1917. He says his fictitious "Hunt County" was somewhat modeled on Gibson County, "but not exactly."

"Once my father, Matthew Hillsman Taylor, a lawyer who lived sometimes in Nashville, Memphis and St. Louis, got mad at me for some of the things I wrote," Taylor said. "He thought people could identify my characters. So I try to mix the people and the places up so that they cannot be identified."

One of Taylor's particular skills in short story writing is in the use of his narrator, critics agree. Often the narrator is a young boy who lived in Nashville when Taylor lived here, and went to Wallace School or Vanderbilt University when Taylor went to those schools.

And inevitably the readers assume that Taylor is narrating his own experiences. In a sense, of course, that is true.

"I write about West End because my mother grew up on West End Avenue, near the Cathedral, and it was a familiar neighborhood to me," Taylor said. "I write about it partly because of what she told me and partly out of my own knowledge of it."

Taylor's mother was Katherine Taylor, daughter of Gov. Robert (Bob) Taylor (governor from 1897 to 1899), and she was a great storyteller, with a delightful sense of humor, Peter Taylor said. Her own observations on the mores of Memphis, for instance, with its fast-paced commercialism and emphasis on "progress," in contrast with Nasvhille's more conservative pace delighted him.

Peter Taylor's parents moved in the easy society of a Nashville that gravitated between summers at their cottages at Monteagle or Beersheba and their substantial homes on West End or Franklin Pike.

His own father moved so often, in the course of his legal practice, that they often rented their home. For a while they lived "eight miles out" on Franklin Pike, and "for a while, briefly, we rented Travelers' Rest from the Williams family and lived there."

"I loved that place," Taylor said.

Taylor's father was not only a lawyer, but "a foxhunter, a sportsman," Taylor said. He moved his family [in] Memphis nine times, and in the course of the years there, Taylor sniffed out the distinctive traits of the two Tennessee cities—Nashville cushioned in its gently rolling bluegrass hills, and Memphis cotton-rich on its "flat and sunbaked and endlessly sprawling" environs so closely tied to Mississippi plantations.

He put some of those differences in a story, "The Captain's Son," published in *The New Yorker* on Jan. 12, 1976. In that story, as the son of a wealthy, plantation-owning Memphis couple marries the daughter of a staid Nashville household during the Depression, the conflicts between the two backgrounds come to crashing climax.

The conflict that dominates many of Taylor's stories grows out of the shift of the southern population from country life to city life.

"The real change in the world is represented there," Taylor said during the interview. "When the South rises in industry, there are new elements in family life and mores."

In this newest story, "In the Miro District," Taylor shows three generations involved in the transition: the eighteen-year-old youth who has always lived in the city; his parents, who moved to Nashville from the country and became a part of the solid upper class, settled in one of the big four-bedroom homes in Acklen Park, just off West End Avenue; and the rugged grandfather, who chooses to remain on the farm in "Hunt County," even with all of its inconveniences.

"My people had moved into the city," Taylor said. "They had made the transition from the country to the city. That shift from country to city interests me."

The setting for the story is Nashville in 1925, and the narrator, like Peter Taylor, was 18 years old at the time [Taylor was eight in 1925.]. "The story of the country mouse and the city mouse has been a real influence on my literary life," Taylor said.

Unlike Faulkner, Taylor does not see the plantation man necessarily undone when he shifts to the city.

"I have always thought that men who ran the plantations successfully later ran the cities, when they made the transition," he said.

Taylor, who left Vanderbilt University to enter Kenyon College
when writer-teacher John Crowe Ransom joined the Kenyon faculty,
received his degree there. Winner of many awards in the literary field,
he has had several collections of his short stories published in book
form.

This newest story, "In the Miro District," is to be the title story in his
next volume, a book to be published by Knopf on April 7.

Taylor dipped back into Middle Tennessee history for his title to the
days when the Spanish rulers called the area the Miro District in
honor of one of the Spanish governors of Louisiana. (Some map-
makers and historians spelled the word *Mero* and Taylor thought of
using that spelling, he said, but he was afraid it would be confused
with Metro.)

Taylor said he had always preferred Nashville to other Tennessee
cities, "because it has more sense of history, and of course there is the
beautiful countryside."

"But I'm crazy about Memphis," he added. "I go there a lot. It's
like Mississippi—the center of plantation life."

Taylor, who never tires of the conflicts within families—conflicts of
the politest kind, among the "nicest" people—is entertained by the
varying points of view at family gathering places.

"It's fun at Monteagle to see Memphis people and Nashville people
mixing there," he said.

He and the girl he married, Eleanor Ross, met and married at
Monteagle, and they have two children, Katherine and Peter. They
share the hobby of restoring old homes, including three at Monteagle
and Sewanee. One of the houses they have restored is at Charlottesville, Va., where he is on the faculty of the University of Virginia.

"I'd love to live in Nashville now," he said. "With country music
there now, it would be fun to see the contrast between the country
music people and the formal Nashville I knew on Franklin Road."

"I'd love to know how those people feel about country music now.
I'd love to write about it."

About that girl in Grandfather Manley's wardrobe?

"All of the story was garbled except the part about the nightriders
and the earthquake and the Confederate veterans," Taylor said.

"I remember going to Confederate Veterans conventions. Grand-

father Manley, in the story, faced things more realistically toward the
end of the story, after he saw a different set of mores in the city."

"The story shows a certain defeat in the grandfather's life when he
gave in to the mores about him and moved into town. It is sad that
way."

Peter Taylor: A Private World of Southern Writing

Ruth Dean/1977

From *The Washington Star,* 2 October 1977, sec. B, 1, 4.
Reprinted by permission of *The Washington Post.*

The white shingle house, its black shutters thrown back to let in the sun and air, its front wall of white-washed brick enclosing a neat landscape of boxwood and fruit trees, looks inviting.

Except for the semi-exclusiveness of the walled garden, this place seems to enjoy being among its neighbors on this quiet dead-end street in Charlottesville.

Just a few blocks away are the imposing neo-classical University of Virginia buildings that bear the architectural imprint of Thomas Jefferson.

In contrast, this serenely-situated house seems unimportant, almost shy. A reflection perhaps of its occupants? Hardly.

For this is the home of one of America's most gifted short story writers, Peter Taylor, and his equally gifted wife, poetess Eleanor Ross Taylor.

On a warm fall day, Taylor answers the doorbell's summons. The doorway frames all six feet of him—a smile that crinkles the laugh lines around his clear eyes; an easy, mobile mouth. With Southern cordiality, he invites his visitors in and immediately introduces them to his wife. Though urged to join the interview, she prefers to leave him the limelight and exits with the excuse that she has some errands to finish. She is a pretty woman, small and slight (she comes just up to his shoulder) with soft graying hair and a cool reserve that contrasts with his warm rush of words.

As he ushers his visitors into the wood-paneled library and its array of family antiques, portraits and worn Oriental rugs, Taylor explains that with their two children grown, they'd moved from a larger house around the corner into this one a few months ago. Because they'd spent most of the summer in Tennessee, he apologizes for the room's

28

appearance, especially the unsorted book shelves, but it is comfortable. It seems to invite confidences and conversation.

"It was marvelous growing up in Tennessee in the '30s if you
wanted to be a writer," he says as he settled in a wingback chair in
front of a 6-foot-high portrait of his great grandfather Nathaniel
Taylor, who was President Andrew Johnson's commissioner of Indian
affairs.

He reminisces. "Allen Tate taught me freshman English. It was a
great renaissance of letters. . . . Katherine Anne Porter was in and
out. . . . Robert Lowell came down there (to Vanderbilt) to hang
around the writers. Lowell and I went on to Kenyon, then L.S.U."

Lowell's sudden and unexpected death three weeks ago in a New
York cab inbound from the airport and a sojourn in Ireland, deeply
shocked Taylor, even though he knew he'd been in ill health. Now
60, they'd been friends for 40 years since their college days.

"He was just down here to see us in June, before he went to
Maine," Taylor said the day he had to postpone this previously
scheduled interview because of the news. Asked if he wanted a little
more time before it was re-set, he had said, "No, I've been through
the worst. Life must go on. I must keep busy."

Now, a week later, the conversation touches on Lowell only after
an hour's talk about other things—Taylor's work, his Tennessee
forebears, his children, and naturally, other writers.

"I've just been reading through more than 100 letters I exchanged
with him," Taylor says. "In them, he makes comments on what I've
written. Yes," he affirms, "I think I'll write a long memoir of him. I'll
use some of these letters." Then leaning forward, he confides, his
voice a little husky, "You know he was a marvelous letter writer. And
what few people knew outside our group of friends was that he had
one of the greatest senses of humor I've ever seen."

Taylor is no slouch himself when it comes to the humor department. His talk is punctuated with witticisms, some of them dry as a
good Pouilly Fume. The conversation has turned to his family, to his
now grown children trying their wings in the career world. His
daughter Katherine's new lifestyle now embraces writing as well as
running a small dairy farm in southwestern Virginia. His son Peter has
just graduated from the university and wants to be a writer as well as
a librarian.

"Both my children want to write; it makes me nervous," he
confesses. Yet, he can laugh at the incongruity of "telling my
students, 'live your life while you're young,' while telling my own
children 'work, preferably at some secure occupation like banking.' "

As to their literary strivings, he worries aloud: "Parents have a right
to be concerned for their children becoming writers. So many go
through life without achieving success."

It reminded him of his own youth, he admits. His father wanted
him to study law and took a pretty dim view of his literary ambitions.
"That was our finest battle," he jokes. "I don't think I would have
been a good lawyer. He finally forgave me."

You can tell Taylor would have been unhappy doing anything else,
for the language is his first love. You can feel it in his writing, in his
tightly constructed sentences, in the poetic cadence of his words. As
he speaks—softly, rapidly, fervently—his thoughts flow as simply as
he writes. His enthusiasm never seems to flag. He loves to talk.

"In the '30s, it wasn't hard to get into school if you had the
money," he remembers, "but it was tougher getting through, perhaps
not by today's standards. I managed to skip whatever I could of
math," he laughs. "Today there's a different kind of toughness;
students are expected to be more mature. In the old days, you could
get by just by telling the life of the author. And it's much harder to be
a professor today because it's a much more respected profession.
Salaries for instance. We used to think of it as an underpaid
professional. For my first job of teaching in 1947, I got paid $2,500.
Sometimes I think it's a scandal how much I'm paid now!

"There were no better writers than (John Crowe) Ransom and
Cleanth Brooks, but writers were not exactly made to feel welcome
by the Ph.D.s. Even creative writing courses were considered extra-
curricular for a long time by the East coast universities. Now writers
have a much better time of it. Even here at the University of Virginia.
We've just had a chair endowed here with a $600,000 donation in
memory of Henry Hoins, the New York publisher. That means we
will have many more fellows here engaged in creative writing. In the
late '30s they did it on a shoestring. Most of those writers were
scholars. Ransom and Robert Penn Warren, with whom I studied at
L.S.U., were Rhodes Scholars. But they didn't have tenure."

Surrounded from the beginning, as it were, by writers, Taylor seems to have been predestined for writing greatness, though fame so far seems to have eluded him except for preceptive critics who've hailed him as a modern Chekhov (he doesn't think so), and the faithful contingent of *New Yorker* readers to whom he's become a household word over the years.

The magazine has published most of the author's short stories which subsequently have found more enduring pre-eminence between book covers as *A Long Fourth and Other Stories, The Widows of Thornton, Miss Leonora When Last Seen, The Collected Stories of Peter Taylor,* and this year, *In the Miro District.* The brilliance of their literary architecture invests them with a permanence as fitting as the Jeffersonian marble monuments wherein Taylor teaches creative writing to a new generation of Southern writers. He can only hope their discoveries and experiences are as exciting as were his own.

Taylor studied under Tate in the spring of 1936 at Southwestern University in Memphis where his family had moved after previous residences in Nashville and St. Louis. Then he entered Vanderbilt that fall to study with Ransom and there became friends with the late poet Randall Jarrell. It set the course for his personal and literary life, for eventually he was to meet his future wife in the home of Tate and his wife, writer Caroline Gordon. They were married in June, 1943 in St. Andrew's School Chapel in Monteagle, Tenn. by Father James Harold Flye, the friend whom writer James Agee *(Death in the Family)* addressed in his famous letter about the school.

When Ransom left Vanderbilt to go to Kenyon College (in Ohio), Jarrell, and later Taylor and Lowell followed him there. Lowell was a transfer student from Harvard, and graduated in the class of 1940 with Taylor. It was their association at Kenyon that began their lifelong friendship of back-and-forth summer visits and mutual literary criticism.

He is reminded of two poems Lowell wrote to him, one in his Pulitzer Prize-winning *Lord Weary's Castle,* and another, of more personal sentiment, in Lowell's *Notebook 67–68.* It recalls school days inspired by "that doleful Kenyon snapshot" of Taylor apparently bedded down with the flu. With a wistful grin, Taylor confirms, "I still have that snapshot. Oh, that was when we were young, and had long hair."

One of Taylor's favorite Lowell stories concerned himself. He was

attending a Washington party shortly after Lowell's celebrated turn-
down of the late President Lyndon Johnson's invitation to receive the
Medal of Freedom at a White House ceremony "because he felt the
whole business of government inviting writers and artists to receive
special recognition was manipulative." When he defended Lowell's
action to a society reporter, he chuckled in memory, "she really gave
me a dressing down. I guess she was a friend of the President's."
More seriously, he says he concurred with Lowell's views; in fact he
doesn't even like the idea of a Council on the Arts "because I think it
leads to the support of mediocrity in the arts because of the basic
premise of providing state grants on a quota system. It just doesn't
work that way in reality. Everyone knows the majority of artists are
concentrated in New York and the New England states."

Did he think friendships between writers, between artists, an
important ingredient of their creative output? "Yes, I think closeness
to other writers is important, certainly the mutual exchange of
criticism as well as praise," though he recalls William Faulkner
"couldn't stand to be around other writers."

Tayor adds sympathetically, "Writers have to protect themselves.
Some are brusque. Ransom was just the opposite. He was so polite
that if strangers approached him, he'd just 'polite' them to death.

"Hemingway had to protect himself too. I've never had that
problem. I noticed in Boston, when I was walking down the street
with Lowell, people would stop him for his signature."

And what of the paradox of his own success, really success without
acclaim? At least the kind that brings the public knocking down your
door, talk show lionizing and autographs on demand.

That kind of acclaim really holds no appeal for Taylor. "It doesn't
bother me much. I've lived among literary people so much of my life,
and had admiration for them, and they for my work, that the other
doesn't matter.

"I don't judge my literary friends by whose name is on the best-
seller list. My wife and I enjoy our circle of friends which include
young writers, some 40 years younger than me. I don't feel the age
difference in the slightest. That was the marvelous thing about Robert
Frost. He'd just take up where we left off. He was sort of gruff; sort of
played that part. At least he knew the impression he was making."

As for his own aspirations, Taylor says, "I always felt I wanted my writing to have a career, but not me. I never wanted to be a culture-hero. You want your writing to have influence on the better, younger writers.

"I think you can't much worry about acclaim. The '60s broke down the distinctions between high and lowbrow. A concert once meant listening to Beethoven and Brahms. Now it's a happening. The same is true of literature. A lot of people are talked about seriously who are pop artists. The slick magazines are gone. Television has taken over. We have to re-classify. I think writing short fiction is much nearer to poetry, than for instance, a novel. It must be very tightly written. Everything has to be saying two or three things at once. A lyric poem must be doing more work than a novel. You can't sustain the intensity in a novel that you do in a short story. You have to sustain the intense use of language. Faulkner does it.

"A story suggests, and a novel has to tell.

"When you put aside a good story by Turgenev, it suggests many things that make you feel as if you'd put down a novel. Katherine Anne Porter is a master of it. Her 'Old Mortality' means much more than most novels. As a matter of fact, I think most novels could be stories. They are so long, they could be more dramatically effective if they were stories."

Taylor tried writing a novel. Really tried. But in the end, tore it up "because I thought it would be boring." The attempt at the longer genre, in fact, short-circuited his usual creative output for about five years. Finally, it was settled, he recalls, "when I woke up in the middle of the night and said, 'you don't have to write that novel.' From that moment, I felt the greatest release. And shortly thereafter, I started writing stories again."

His newest book, *In the Miro District,* contains four stories written as poems. "I've often written stories in meter," Taylor observes, as though that were the easiest way in the world to exercise one's literary prerogatives. In fact that's how he wrote the first and last stories in the book, "then put them back in prose. It's fun."

Writing should be a joy, he believes. "I think it shows if a writer hasn't had fun, if he hasn't been excited by it and gotten ideas as he goes along. Through writing, you learn what you think."

His first stories were about the people he knew in his life, his Southern relatives and their black servants. The stories didn't win him great understanding. "People thought me anti-black, or condescending," he explains, "when what I was trying to do was to win sympathy for the black people I wrote about by portraying them exactly as the human beings they were, and contrasting what the Southern white attitudes were about them. Otherwise I would have been portraying them as symbols."

Far from being condescending, Taylor believes his writing does have a social consciousness. But the causes, "are very quiet—not the kind that wave the flag or lead us over the barricades. I guess I'm too subtle for some to get my meanings," he muses.

As an example, he mentions a story he wrote called, "Who Was Jesse's Friend and Protector?" It is about a black man who worked for an "overly refined white couple." Away from his employers, the man led a dissolute life. On his return, he talked about his jaunts on visits to the couple, and they took vicarious pleasure in hearing about them. But the story ends on a sad note. The black man is ultimately destroyed by his life, on the tales of which this couple has so greedily feasted.

This is a more extreme denouement than some of Taylor's other stories, but all possess this quality of the unusual lurking beneath the surface of the usual—whether it's the hidden attitudes forced to surface because of a quirkish turn of events like a locked-in bathroom situation which terrifies a new bride in "Reservations," or a puritanical upbringing which ironically spells doom for a hapless relative in "The Hand of Emmagene," one of the stories in Taylor's most recent book.

"Reservations," incidentally, was made into a television play 10 years ago on the U.S. Steel Hour, "but they changed the ending," Taylor complained. He is happy, however, that some of his other works, which incidentally include a fair sampling of short plays, have awakened more recent interest in televising them. Nothing definite as yet.

With an amused smile, he comments, "If I had wanted to make a killing on this last book, I could have stretched out any of those stories to 200 pages and made it into a novel. A book of short stories never makes money—not as much as any one story in *The New Yorker!* I've published only one novel, *A Woman of Means.* But it's not as good as my stories."

Peter Taylor Remembers Robert Lowell

Robert Wilson/1982

From *Washington Post Book World,* 14 November 1982, 1, 8.
©1982 by *The Washington Post.* Reprinted by permission.

In the fall of 1937 Peter Taylor and Robert Lowell trans-
ferred to Kenyon College in Ohio to study under the poet
and critic John Crowe Ransom. Lowell, a Northerner,
wanted to be a poet, and Taylor, a Southerner, wanted to
be a fiction writer (his *Collected Stories* were published in
1969; his most recent book of stories is *In the Miro
District*). They became great and lifelong friends. In his
comfortable house in Charlottesville, where he teaches at
the University of Virginia, Peter Taylor talked recently
about his old friend with *Book World* assistant editor
Robert Wilson.

Robert Wilson: I wonder almost that you could have wanted to be
friends with the young Robert Lowell. In [Ian Hamilton's biography],
as a young man, he seems not to be a terribly appealing person. He
seems to match his nickname, Cal, which was in part for Caliban,
wasn't it?

    Peter Taylor: Caligula.

    RW: Wasn't it both Caligula and Caliban? That's what the biogra-
phy says.

    PT: They say other things now, but I was always told it was for
Caligula. He was crazy about the Romans. . . .

    RW: Well, at any rate, he seemed a kind of Caliban-like creature.

    PT: He was not unappealing as a person, but he was awful
looking. He never cut his hair, he never took a bath. His shoes often
had the soles divided, and were just flapping. He looked terrible.
Though he had what he called his good suit, which hung in our

35

closet at Kenyon always, as a sort of sacred object. But he was such a dominant type that anyone whose acquaintance he wanted he could get.

RW: When you first met him, did you feel that you were going to be friends, that you wanted to be friends?

PT: I found him to be very interesting. I've always been attracted to people who are not like me—it's the "not me in thee" I like. He was so totally different. He was the intellectual and a poet and a classicist. I admired from the beginning his determination to get to know the people he thought were the most talented. He wanted to find out what was best in literature, and he was always pursuing that, and not rejecting anything until he'd really explored it. I admired all of that in him.

But, right after college, he went with me to Memphis, he and Jean (Stafford, the late novelist and short-story writer)—they had married while he was still in college—to stay with my family. . . .

RW: He seems like the last person you'd want to take home to meet your parents.

PT: But my parents found him attractive, and he was crazy about my mother. Anyone who excelled in any way she was attracted to and wanted to respond to. And he had a great way of making jokes and teasing, and right away they got into it. My parents and my sister—all the people who met him—liked him, and he would make an effort to win people, and he could. Because he had this very silly streak and he liked to make fun and joke.

RW: Was he a good student? Apparently he was rather indifferent about Harvard. Then suddenly we find him graduating from Kenyon first in his class.

PT: He had been a wonderful student at St. Mark's (school). He hadn't been sure, at that age, if he'd wanted to be a writer. He was interested in painting, or at least in talking about painting. And history, that was his great interest. Then at Harvard—he hated the superficial—and he got the feeling that Harvard was . . . Harvard. Not for him. Then also, you have to admit that he was not a very important person at Harvard.

He was almost a recluse. Even when I knew him at Kenyon. Then, after he became famous and acclaimed—I've noticed this about other people—he changed completely. He became much more gregarious than I, and wanted to be the center of things, and admired. Well, that's just the way people are. And that was irksome, to some extent. At Kenyon, he didn't drink, he didn't go out with girls. He was just a big school-boy.

RW: What about his poetry? Hamilton seems almost to make fun of his early poems?

PT: As an undergraduate? Well, all his teachers thought it was extremely obvious that he was going to be a poet. The poems were awkward, and they were pedantic at times. But he was always interested in working on form, on mastering form. And this is what I have observed in him more than in anybody else, I think: his work habits, and his determination to rewrite. He would write poems in those days over and over, and some of the poems that he wrote then, that are very long and difficult and . . . inchoate . . . I laugh when I say that because he used that word when we were undergraduates to tease me. He quoted one of the professors at Kenyon who had read something I'd written and had said that it was inchoate. That infuriated me, because I didn't really quite know what it meant.

But he would rework things and make you read them in every version, and he would read my work. He had read almost no fiction, and we began reading fiction aloud, and making an anthology of poetry together. We read the 17th-century poets to choose for the anthology, and he made all the choices. But our tastes coincided a lot—almost always—and he was responsive to my ideas. But we would fight. We had real fights about literary things, but it was because we were both so opinionated.

What I was going to say was he would write long poems that were not successful as poetry, but then later, much later, lines and sections of those early poems would appear. I have a lot of his early manuscripts, you see. (He shows photocopies of these manuscripts.) On the front are his poems in longhand. This just takes me back. I had to read pages and pages of this, and go over it line for line. Then on the back—he was on the football team at Kenyon—and on the back were football plays. He would just write on any piece of paper: this was just a nice big piece of paper to write on. He played tackle, because he was so big.

But the thing he had to teach other poets—others of his genera-tion—more than anything else was this business of rewriting and experimenting. You can see how in different versions of poems he would change the entire meaning. He'd get carried away by a line. He was objective the way a writer has to be. Finally the form would take over the poem and the idea would just develop.

. . . He had a horror of being commonplace, of not being distinguished amongst the best. Well, that's a terrible trait. I mean it makes you hard to live with. It makes you a snob. And he *was* a little bit. But on the other hand, it was his great forte. He wouldn't have been happy to be just a good poet. For him it was the old saying, "The good is the enemy of the best." I think he really felt like that.

RW: Lowell became famous in part for his letters to Presidents Roosevelt and Johnson protesting their respective wars. But was he very interested in politics, really?

PT: When we were young he was not interested in politics at all. None of us was at Kenyon, except (Randall) Jarrell. And he knew nothing about politics. Lowell would say things like, "Someday after college I'll go to New York, maybe, and become a Communist for a time, and learn about politics." And then he'd say, "I'll go to London and learn how to dress." He really said those things. But that's the way he was about everything. He was a learner. He imagined that all life was made up of compartments and that he would go into each of them and learn everything about them and finally put the whole thing together.

RW: In Hamilton's biography Lowell seems to go from his crackups to periods of recovery, but then he seems to have gotten completely well. Was there any cumulative effect of all these spells?

PT: No, I would see him at times when he was just the way he'd always been. But when he had his first crackup, it was at my house in Indiana, where I was teaching then. We went for a walk the afternoon he got there; as a matter of fact I was trying to keep him away from my house. And he was saying such outrageous things. Oh, we talked as always about . . . literature. I remember talking to him about Thomas Wolfe. I'd been reading Thomas Wolfe again, and I was expressing some ideas that I wouldn't agree with now. He was interested; he hadn't read Thomas Wolfe at all. But he began saying such outrageous things that I began to see that he really was insane. It had such a terrible effect on me. Because then all the long talks we'd had, even years at school, and after—I just felt that he'd been insane always. I nearly cracked up myself. It was as though I'd been deluded all those years. But then when I saw him again he was himself.

RW: What about his friendship with Randall Jarrell? There's a suggestion in the biography that he held Jarrell off as a friend a little bit because he valued him so much as a critic.

PT: I don't think he held him off. He considered Jarrell a great friend. They were tempermentally different, but they found their difference interesting. And their lives were different. When Cal came to visit in Greensboro (where Taylor and Jarrell were teaching), he would spend just as much time with Jarrell as he did with me. And he and Jarrell would go over Cal's newest poems. But Jarrell, if he liked your effort, would write you a long letter about it, and if he didn't he wouldn't speak to you. Cal had exactly that experience, too, and we would laugh about it.

RW: You said earlier that Lowell liked to joke and be silly. Did he have a sense of humor?

PT: I must say he had a rather strange sense of humor. Ian Hamilton's book, for all its virtues—and I do think that it's a very fine biography, that Hamilton does the essential thing of relating the poetry to the life, and does it wonderfully well—shows little awareness and no real understanding of his special brand of humor. His humor was often childish, often corny, sometimes no less than sick. Yet I always liked his jokes—except of course when they were at my expense. He invented facts and stories that made his dearest friends out as clichés of whatever they really were—cliché Jews, cliché Southerners, cliché Englishmen. Naturally this was irksome sometimes—even mischief-making. He was fond of representing me as a Southern racist, though of course he knew better—knew it from the hours of talk we had had on the subject, as well as from my published stories. We didn't quarrel about it, though. We never quarreled about anything after we left college.

Anyhow, the biography doesn't interpret or attempt to deal very much with his humor, and the result is that, with all the book's careful delineation of his madness, there is the danger of his being seen as an unrelieved grotesque. None of his friends saw him as that—not one of them. His teasing was often rough, but he was the most affectionate and loyal of friends. And I might add that he expected teasing and affection and loyalty *from* his friends. And so that really made the teasing and the outrageous inventions all right with us. Actually, it was his way of drawing closer to his friends, rather than putting them off.

RW: He wrote some wonderful, generous letters to other poets, especially when they were having bad times. Jarrell. John Berryman. And he was also very kind to Ezra Pound, very loyal to him. What was that from? Was that because Pound was sort of an elder statesman?

PT: Yes, I was just thinking that. Pound was the great poet. Of course Lowell did admire him and admire his work. Pound was one of his models as a poet, and he was attracted to him for that.

Part of it was Lowell's really being kind, but always, with people's kindness, it's a mixture, it's because they want to feel themselves kind. He did enjoy Pound. Pound was the most eccentric man alive. They put Pound in a madhouse because they didn't know what else to do with him. They didn't want to put him in jail. And, as people said, Pound was no madder than he'd ever been.

RW: But Lowell did keep up.

PT: Well, he had a strong sense of father-son relationship, and this was one of his problems and one of his virtues. He liked the relationship with Ford Madox Ford, with Allen Tate, with Ransom. . . .

RW: And T. S. Eliot and William Carlos Williams?

PT: Oh, very much. And Frost. All of those older people. He liked that relationship with them. But it was because they—it was one of his virtues—he learned from them, and he admired them, and the things he admired he wanted to protect and be near.

The Inspired Voice of Mythical Tennessee
Robert Daniel/1983

From *Kenyon College Alumni Bulletin,* 7 (Winter 1983), 18–20.
© 1983 by Kenyon College. Reprinted by permission.

Daniel: Could you talk about your appointment to the American Academy of Arts and Letters? Is it like L'academie Francais?

Taylor: It thinks of itself as so.

Daniel: Does it try to affect the language?

Taylor: Not that I know of. I've just been elected, and I don't go to meetings often. I really can't tell you much about it, except that it mostly gives prizes and awards to young writers. Also, members give papers and readings, and music people present concerts. They have an incredible building way uptown in Manhattan—it's enormous with art galleries and auditoriums and dining facilities. But there are no dues or anything like that.

Daniel: What are you working on now?

Taylor: I'm working on what I call a book-length story. I won't say the other word. But I am, and I have been now for about a year. I don't have the same ideas about work that some people do. I don't believe in working, you know. I do my writing the way ladies do their knitting. I just have it around handy, when there's an odd moment. I have done a little this morning.

The main thing is that I work differently at different points in a story. At certain parts in the story—toward the end, for example—I work around the clock. But I don't believe that people ought to produce stories or poems the way they produce automobiles. I don't really believe in professionalism. It's one of the subjects about which I'm rabid. Some people think they have to turn out a story or a book a year to be a writer in the professional sense. They're careerists, really. I write whenever I get an idea. I may get an idea in the night and get up to write on it. When I get up in the morning my first thought is, "Will I write anything today?" And usually I do make a few notes. I look at my manuscripts first thing every morning and I

41

may write on them. I don't think I'm a professional or an amateur; I think I'm an inspired idiot. I just write. As they say in the country, "I do like I know."

Daniel: You say manuscripts. Are you working on more than one now?

Taylor: Yes. As a matter of fact I like to write on several things at the same time. I have three long manuscripts that I've done lots of work on—maybe 100 pages on each. In the past I've always written stories 50 pages or under. But those have stretched out, and I've gotten very much involved in one of them for a period of time. Need I say it's all in Tennessee? It takes place in Nashville and Memphis and Chattanooga. They are not the real cities of Memphis and Nashville and Chattanooga. They're mythical cities. I don't worry about whether I'm portraying them right; I have these cities that are useful to me, representing certain values and certain things. It's based largely on my father's life and my relationship to my father. I get involved in something like that, and for days I'll think about that. I think writing is discovery. You discover what you know about something or what you feel about things. For me it is this way. Instead of setting out with some social idea or scene or something, I discover what I think about something by writing. I've always done that. I've discovered all sorts of motives, for instance, in my father's life and in my own and in other people's. One of the great delights of it is not having to tell the literal truth. You wander off and imagine how you might have liked it to be. A lot of writing is wishful thinking. You're not bound by scenes, houses, situations. Several people have suggested that I write some memiors about Lowell and Jarrell and Ransom and Tate, and I have no intention of doing that. It's too confining to be writing the truth. But one of my long pieces is about literary people, and I'm writing close to those people.

Daniel: Your fiction is not concerned at all with political or social issues, is it?

Taylor: No, but when I'm writing I discover sometimes what I really think about social issues. I'm not an intellectual except in terms of my fiction. I'll discover what I think of a lot of the issues that people talk about constantly—about the family and what's happened to it and the deterioration and the end of the family as unit in society. I think it is a barbarian dunghill that doesn't have the family unit in the society.

Daniel: But there's no direct expression?

Taylor: Oh, never. Unless I have some character who is interested in that. And I don't have many.

Daniel: I seem to remember your giving yourself a more respectable title than inspired idiot. You referred to yourself as a journeyman writer. What does that mean?

Taylor: I don't know now. There is such a thing as inspiration, and there should be. You could say "inspired artist" instead of "inspired idiot." The distinction is that I am not a career man, like a lawyer or a doctor. Not at all. And people often make that comparison. I remember Delmore Schwartz once saying of Caroline Gordon, "I don't like her work very much, but she's a real professional." And that seems to be the opposite of what you want people to say. I would rather hear someone say, "He's not a professional, but in this work he was really inspired."

Daniel: You make it sound as if you write very casually, but in fact, you've been very productive.

Taylor: That's another point. I think you should write as much as you feel the impulse to write and as long as you derive great pleasure from it. And I always have. It's the thing I enjoy most in the world. I don't think it's hard work. I've done it all my life. And I think that people who drive themselves to get something on paper, to write— well, they may turn into a Tolstoy, or they may not. They may turn out to be nothing. It's what comes from inside, or the person's intellect, that determines it. You can't make yourself into a writer. It seems an absurdity, unless it's a degree in the teaching of writing.

Daniel: But you have to give grades to your students, don't you?

Taylor: I do. And the only reason I do, is that I once tried to give only pass-fail credit, and it turned out to be unfair to some people who were the really gifted writers in the class. Often these students do not get their best grades in other courses, and it seemed they were being penalized by not getting credit for the thing they did best. So I reverted to giving grades, which are nonsensical. I think you can't really grade a piece of writing. There's no comparison, no scale or curve.

Daniel: If you're going to give grades, then you have to have deadlines.

Taylor: I tell them that I do that as a favor to them. It's a favor to them to have a deadline, to have to get a piece of work done, because they have other demands on them. I remember putting my writing off to the last. If you have to have deadlines in other courses, then you had better have one in creative writing, or you won't ever find the time for it.

Daniel: Back to your own work. You seem to have been more productive in writing short stories than novels.

Taylor: Absolutely. I'm not a novelist. These pieces I'm writing now are long short stories. I really think Mr. Ransom is partly responsible for that. When I was at Kenyon, there were all these poets around, and I tried to write poetry. Writing a short story depends a lot on compression. That's the main way to differentiate it from a novel. In writing with Ransom, every emphasis was on compression. When you write poetry, you have to make a word count for more, a line count for more. In a certain way a short story is somewhere between a novel and a poem. Chekhov's stories are really poems. The best stories can be talked about as poems in the same way. You see the structure, you see it all at once, as you can't in the novel.

Daniel: There was a review in the *New York Times* that referred to you as the American Chekhov. Do you agree?

Taylor: No, no, no. I don't agree. I would love to agree. I read a lot of Chekhov when I was young, and very few people do read Chekhov. People talk about him. I used to say I would ask people in an English department, "Who is the greatest short story writer?" and they'd say, "Chekhov." And I'd say, "Tell me five of his stories." And very few of them could tell me five stories by Chekhov. So he's not read. But I did read him, and I learned compression from him, but I don't have his poetic talent.

Daniel: Would you say your objectives in writing a story are different from his?

Taylor: Sometimes and sometimes not. I turned in recent years to writing a lot of short stories in the sort of broken line prose that looks like free verse. It's, again, an effort to compress. When you do that, you get more out of a line. The end of the line is significant. You get the syntax of poetry and the ordinary syntax of prose. You're seeing more in a short space. You can have a run-on line that will be significant. And that's what I've been trying for. To make the language count, to make every word, every sentence, count more. If you have a run-on sentence, the comparison of the last half of one sentence and the beginning of the next says something, or should. It does in a poem, and it does in a story. I've tried always to find ways of writing very short stories and getting a great deal of compression in them. Because a short story should say as much and be as good as a long story, as a novel. Otherwise you would have to say a novel is greater than a lyric poem. And no one would say that. There is so much more compression in a lyric poem.

Daniel: When you write a story in free-verse, so to speak, do you leave it like that for publication?

Taylor: Sometimes I do. I've printed a good many like that. Some I don't. I write everything that way—even these book-length stories. I write first in that way because it makes me give a lot more attention to the interest of the line and the phrase. But if it gets very long and the line length—the breaking of the line—seems to have no significance, then I reconvert. Sometimes when I get to the end of the story, I get exhausted trying to give intrinsic interest to each line. But I'll go and finish it that way. "In the Miro District," and "The Captain's Son" are long stories that I wrote first in this other way. Even the long "Old Forest" I wrote first in this form (It's not in any book yet. It's set in Memphis; the man is engaged to one girl but is out with another kind of girl in the park, and they have an accident. By the way, they're making a film of that, in Memphis right now, and I'm having a lot of fun with that.). If the stories bog down—and I can usually realize it— then I put them in regular prose form. When I sent "The Gift of the Prodigal" to *The New Yorker* in free verse, they said they would print it, but they wanted me to put it in regular prose form. Well, I did, but when I put it back in a book, I'm going to return it to the other form. I don't call it free verse because it's not free verse. It's not that strict. I used to be horrified, when I was very young, at anybody writing poetic fiction or free verse prose—work not strictly one or the other. Mr. Ransom used to feel that way, I guess. I've come to think, "What difference does it make?" Anything you can get that works is good.

Daniel: While we're on the subject of the different forms, that you've tried, you've written four plays. Are you tempted to write any more?

Taylor: Oh, absolutely. And I'm going to. But the theater is the graveyard of fiction writers. I enjoy doing them. I've never had a New York production, of course, but I have had them in college theaters and little theaters. When somebody is going to put one on, I go hurrying off to see it, and to work with them, because I love doing it. Jim Michael (professor emeritus of drama) was the best director I ever had. He gave me for several years what anyone who wants to write plays needs—a director who likes the plays, understands them, and just tells you, "You give us the play, and we'll do it." And that was marvelous for me those years when my plays were done at Kenyon. It was great fun and very satisfying to me. I learned more from that than from anything.

Daniel: What are the chances for a young writer? Is it harder to get published now?

Taylor: Well, I think it is. Magazine publication is harder, anyway. For one thing, there are so many more writers, and there are fewer literary magazines. The *Kenyon* and the *Sewanee* and the *Partisan* and the *Southern* don't have the authority that they once had, for some reason. I don't believe it's the fault of the magazines. When I was young, if you did get published in those magazines, everybody you cared about seeing your work saw it. Well now there are a lot of little magazines, and the young people I know don't read them as much. Also the big magazines have tried to draw off a lot of the good young writers, and they'll publish them and want them to change things, and the young writers, eager to publish, will do that. I think it is very hard for them now. I don't know what they can do except go on publishing in little magazines. Publishing of books is just a terrible situation, everybody in New York tells me. Big corporations own the publishing houses now, and they want them to make money. Poetry and fiction that's not going to be a best seller have a very hard time. There are only two publishers, I think, that are not owned by corporations—Farrar Straus & Giroux and Houghton-Mifflin. Those big businessmen are telling them, "Don't publish what won't sell." And a lot of good, young writers' work won't sell at first. Later they create their own public. But that's not the way to run a publishing house.

Daniel: And the same thing applies to volumes of short stories, I suppose?

Taylor: Oh, it's terrible. Of course, it's always been bad. Poets have each other, and novelists have potentially a mass audience, but short story writers have nothing. People talk about it being the American form, but it is not a thing that is read as much as either poetry or fiction. At least the poets have an articulate reader or audience.

Daniel: Finally, could you speak briefly on the Southern tradition? Do you see yourself as a part of that? Or is that tradition diminishing? Is it as strong as ever?

Taylor: For me it is, because I grew up in it and all my teachers were Southerners and Southern writers. It was one of those marvelous coincidences in life that I grew up with very strong Southern feelings in my family and in my interests—temperamentally—and then just at the right psychological moment I came under the influence of Tate, Ransom and Warren. That was very important in my life. The world is changing constantly, and the South is disappearing, really, but there will still be young writers who will come along and be interested in who they are, and be temperamentally disposed to write about that, and be influenced by older writers. I meet them all the time. Sometimes I meet young writers at the University of Virginia who are very Southern, who are just violent in their feelings. And I almost feel sorry for them, because so much of what they're interested in has disappeared. But on the other hand, there's worlds of it there still. There will be country boys or girls from Southside Virginia, who'll be be just mad about Southern history and about the cultural differences of the South. And they will write.

Peter Taylor: Writing, Teaching and Making Discoveries
Robert Brickhouse/1983

From *University of Virginia Alumni News*, 72 (November/December 1983), 14–16. Copyright © 1983 by University of Virginia Alumni Association. Reprinted by permission.

A few years after he moved to Charlottesville, Peter Taylor happened to discover among some family papers an ancient letter that revealed an ancestor of his had lived nearby, along the Rivanna River in the early 1800s.

There shouldn't be anything too surprising about that coincidence, Mr. Taylor says, putting a visitor immediately at ease by offering this family anecdote. "*Everybody* in Tennessee came originally from either North Carolina or Virginia."

Peter Hillsman Taylor, son of Tennessee, teacher, and teller of stories, retired in June after 16 years on the faculty of the University of Virginia.

Although he has taught at several universities over the years, including Oxford, Harvard and Chicago, "the students here are the best I've ever had," he says in his distinctly Southern accent. "They're the best for what I teach: writing."

Retirement for Mr. Taylor means retirement only from the regular teaching of writing. As one of the America's most respected fiction writers himself—he is considered a master of the short story form— he plans to travel to accept some of the many invitations he has received to be a guest lecturer, and he will no doubt continue to teach a course here from time to time, he says.

And mornings still find the 66-year-old Mr. Taylor doing what he has been doing most mornings of his life: "at least thinking about my writing."

When he is in Charlottesville, this happens in a downstairs study at

48

his home on Wayside Place, a tree-shaded street a few blocks from
the University.

Mr. Taylor does his writing with a pencil in a notebook. He doesn't
like the increasingly popular word-processors that enable writers to
string their words rapidly across a computer screen. "I think writing
should be slow," he says. "I wrote seven pages in one day recently,
and for me that was phenomenal."

Last year, Mr. Taylor, following in the footsteps of such writers as
William Dean Howells, Mark Twain and Henry James, was elected to
the American Academy of Arts and Letters, the highest recognition of
artistic merit in the country. Membership is limited to 50 persons who
are chosen by the National Institute of Arts and Letters and who hold
their chairs for life.

Over the last 40 years, he has published seven volumes of stories
and short fiction, including *The Widows of Thornton, Happy Families
Are All Alike, In the Miro District* and a *Collected Stories,* as well as
several books of plays and a novel, *A Woman of Means.* Many of the
stories have appeared in *The New Yorker* or in such small-press
journals as *The Sewanee Review, Kenyon Review* and *Shenandoah.*

More than once compared to Chekhov in his crafting of stories, Mr.
Taylor has drawn to the University a generation of students who
came to study writing with him. John Casey, a novelist who was
encouraged to follow a writing career by Mr. Taylor and who now
teaches fiction here, once said of him: "At a casual meeting you'd
really have no idea that this amiable, attractive, sociable man who
happily endorses all sorts of pleasant social conventions, is in fact a
demon radical spoiling certain young men and women for ordinary
lives. . . . He can call spirits from the vasty deep. . . . Peter calls them
in a cheerful voice, and they come."

Many of Mr. Taylor's stories are set in his native Tennessee and
often involve the genteel ways of upper-middle-class families, the sort
of world he himself was born into. But, as the critic Jonathan Yardley
has written, "the dramas that take place within them are univer-
sal. . . . Taylor is a regionalist only to the extent that he uses the
territory he knows best as the bedrock upon which to rest work that
ranges far afield in its larger subjects."

"I maintain that writing is how you discover what you think," Mr.
Taylor says, answering an interviewer's question about what is in-

volved in the process. He has spent part of the day working at the current one of the many old Albemarle County houses that he and his wife, the poet Eleanor Ross Taylor, have made a hobby of restoring. A tall, trim man, Mr. Taylor has changed into a freshly pressed blue pinstriped shirt and slacks and is sitting on a sofa by a window.

"I didn't know what I thought about blacks, for example, until I started writing about them—and saw that they got the short end of it. And I didn't know what I thought about women. Often you won't know what you think. That's why people write about their families so much."

Born in Trenton, Tenn., the son of a lawyer, Mr. Taylor was raised in Nashville and Memphis, and relatives from throughout the state gave the family connections to both country and city in several sections. He heard stories at home from as early as he can remember.

"Most Southern families are always telling stories," he says. In such tales of family or local incidents, "often people tell them using the same words again and again." "In The Miro District," the long title story of the 1977 volume of the same name, for example, includes a true tale he heard his grandfather tell about being kidnapped by hooded nightriders during the Civil War.

Mr. Taylor's mother was especially, he says, "a wonderful story-teller. My father would love to hear my mother tell stories—he'd often get her to tell the one about such and such." In this family setting, it was natural that "from the time I was a little boy I made up stories for myself."

When his urge to write took a serious turn, he went to study with Allen Tate, the poet and critic, at Southwestern at Memphis. Tate, says Mr. Taylor, "was the best teacher I ever had. He made literature seem important."

Tate has written of Mr. Taylor: "The simple truth is that he did not need to know anything I could teach him. He had a perfection of style at the age of 18 that I envied."

Mr. Taylor later went to Kenyon College in Gambier, Ohio, where he studied with the poet John Crowe Ransome and received a B.A. in 1940. The poets Robert Lowell and Randall Jarrell, who were to become life-long friends of Mr. Taylor until their deaths, also were students at Kenyon at the time. Mr. Taylor's story "1939," about a youthful journey that two Kenyon students make to New York, is in some ways a portrait of himself and Lowell, he acknowledges. "Jarrell used to say I ought just to have used the real names."

Mr. Taylor later went to Louisiana State to do graduate work with Robert Penn Warren but soon dropped out to devote full time to writing. After serving in the Army, he began teaching writing and held posts at several colleges, including Kenyon and Indiana University. He was on the faculty of the University of North Carolina at Greensboro [off and on] from 1946 to 1967, when he was offered an endowed professorship in English at Virginia.

"When I first started teaching, I never dreamed I'd be doing it all my life," he says. And when he received an invitation to teach here, he recalls, his father and brother, at home in Tennessee, were enthusiastic. Although they had taken note of his teaching at Oxford and Harvard along the way, "they were most impressed about my coming to *the* University."

And, as it turned out, "the University treated me well. They let me do what I wanted to do. I've been lucky, because I've been given time to write and allowed to teach writing only. If you have to teach period courses and work on your doctorate, you can't get any writing done. The way I've been treated here is the way to treat writers, if you want to have them around. Don't try to make them into academics."

Mr. Taylor teaches writing partly by reading to his students. He reads stories by writers as various as Tolstoy, Chekhov, James, Faulkner, and Hemingway and examines how their sentences are written. Reading aloud, "you're showing people how writers write," he says, adding that he doesn't believe an art form like fiction-writing can be taught by lecturing about it.

He also teaches in individual conferences, encouraging strong points and tactfully suggesting how to improve weaknesses. As Mr. Taylor puts it, "I've never learned from anything said *against* my stories."

Taking a writing course is important for all literature students, not just those who would be writers, Mr. Taylor believes, because "it teaches about reading. You can learn a great deal about literature by trying to write. A writing course is not necessarily going to make everyone into a writer. But when you get a good writer, you can help him make leaps he wouldn't ordinarily have made."

As for himself, he says, "there's a satisfaction in influencing a young writer's taste." And teaching has been good in another respect too. "When you're a writer, you're by yourself all the time, and you get withdrawn from the world. Teaching draws you out. I'm a gregarious person who likes to see people."

"A real fiction writer," Mr. Taylor says, "has to like to tell and read stories. It's like a compulsion. You don't have to worry about the content—your ideas will come out, just as they do in your dreams." Sometimes when he is writing, he says, "I will at first think there is one theme, and then another theme will almost seem to take over."

People like to hear stories, he believes, because stories "seem to make some order out of the chaos of life. Boy wins girl, so we know he must have been a 'good guy.' That says something about life. Fiction says, 'life is not just chaos: It means something.' You're trying to see sense in events, and you also see how the way things go influences character."

In the course of a story, "the excitement of events" keeps the reader following along, Mr. Taylor says, although when he was younger he thought too much emphasis on plot was "a vulgarity. But now I've come to think of it as important. I'm rather fond of building up a plot now."

A sense of history is important too, he says. "It's a sense of how the past affects the present. That's the reason one can go on writing—to make these discoveries about the past and the present."

He often starts writing about something close to his own life, he says, but then the work will take off on a direction of its own. "If something sticks in my mind for months and years, I know it must be important to me," he says. Unusual incidents or anecdotes, in particular, hold the seeds of his fiction, as in a story he once heard about a human hand found mysteriously in a trash can. The image later evolved into his powerful narrative-verse tale "The Hand of Emmagene."

Although he often begins writing a story with a character, a description or idea in mind, he says, "besides having ideas about your story, you've got to have emotions and feelings—love and hate."

He doesn't outline his story, he says, but "I make so many notes in the margins of the first two pages that it constitutes an outline. I maintain that you get a second inspiration in a story. You think you know what your characters will do—but suddenly it gets more complicated. Characters' motives can completely change in the course of my writing."

"In The Miro District," with its tale he had ruminated on since he was a boy, is about "holding on to values in a changing world," Mr. Taylor says. And in the end, the grandfather in the story, who reverts to playing out the role of Civil War veteran that is forced on him, "is defeated by a changing world."

Today, "many people suddenly find themselves in a world where values are changing fast," Mr. Taylor says. "There are no standards to hold on to. Everything is affected by what happens in Hollywood or New York. People lose their integrity."

How does he keep his on integrity in such a world?

"You write," says Mr. Taylor. "You try to comprehend. You explore the questions that everybody has. In my own small way, that's what I try to do with these stories."

An Interview with Peter Taylor
Don Keck DuPree/1984

From *Touchstone* [Nashville, TN], 1 (Fall 1984), 8, 12. Reprinted by permission.

Preparing an honorary degree citation some years ago, Andrew Lytle wrote: "PETER HILLSMAN TAYLOR was born. When and where (Trenton, Tennessee, 1917) is a matter of biography. This we do know: he is descended from political Taylors in East Tennessee and West Tennessee. His grandfather, his great-grandfather, and his great-uncle ran for Governor at the same time. His great-grandmother took to her bed. Tennessee history calls this the War of the Roses.

"But Mr. Taylor did not follow the family calling. His interest is in the electorate as it reveals all the possible complications of the human condition. His concern is words, not votes. Each of his fictions is a work of art, for he understands the courtship of the deathless Muse. She is timeless, and so must be the garlands the poet lays at her feet. Nothing deformed, but a subject made whole by its form."

One of those fictions, "The Old Forest," is the basis of a new film to be premiered in Memphis on November 2, 1984.

Touchstone asked Taylor about his involvement with the film's making. Passages are taken from the story, first published in *The New Yorker* for May 14, 1979.

> I was already formally engaged, as we used to say, to the girl I was going to marry. But still, I sometimes went out on the town with girls of a different sort.
>
> Nat Ramsey, narrator.

Touchstone: What was your involvement in the film's production?

Taylor: I had no stated part, actually. Steve Ross—he's a very clever man—did the adaptation. I went over the script with him three times—word for word—most of the dialogue comes right out of the story. I really learned a lot about making films, though I was not there for any of the shooting. The editing has taken several months; that's where the real work comes in.

When I was in Sewanee this summer, the crew came up and I did the voice-over narration for the film. I had no training in voice or anything like that. I had to do a lot of retakes, sometimes 15 times. You read it several times and they can take sentences they like best. It was great fun and interesting—sort of an ego trip.

Touchstone: Was this the first time you'd been involved in the filming of one of your stories?

Taylor: Yes. "Reservations" was made into a U.S. Steel Hour several years ago; I had no part in that.

Touchstone: "The Old Forest," as a reminiscence rather than the portrayal of an immediate action, must have posed some tough problems to Ross as he translated it to action before the camera. Did this require the introduction of any new material?

Taylor: No. He did use some scenes from another story. For instance, to give a picture of night life in the joints of Memphis, he took part of the much earlier story "The Other Times."

> It was the kind of place where you had to ring several times before they let you in . . . we had rung the bell the second time and were standing outside under the light, with its private flock of bugs whirling around it, waiting for Aunt Martha to have a look at us through some crack somewhere and decide if she would let us in. . . .
> "The Other Times," *Collected Stories*

Touchstone: In what way is the film version an entirely new work in its own right?

Taylor: It's very close to the story and uses the dialogue. Captures the spirit of it very much. Steve Ross liked the complexity of the story—its different levels of interest. (It's hard for me to be objective about all this; I'm too close to the original story.) Ross knew the story so well—he would say to me, "When you are seeing this, such and such a picture will be on the screen." He doesn't have a messy literary mind; it's all very accurate and clear in his head.

Touchstone: Sounds as though you and Ross got along very well.

Taylor: Oh, yes. He would begin to tell me about the story, then laugh and say, "You already know. . . ." He emphasized certain scenes that appealed to him. As I said before, he's a very clever man.

He knew how to bring the older man alive—knew how to make his
point of view clear.

> As a matter of fact, it was not unusual in those days—forty years ago—for
> a well-brought-up young man like me to keep up his acquaintance, until
> the very eve of his wedding, with some member of what we facetiously
> and somewhat arrogantly referred to as the Memphis demimonde.

Touchstone: The car accident which precipitates this particular
story, occurs as Nat Ramsey and current "female companion"—not
his fiancee—are driving through Overton Park toward Southwestern
where Nat is to study for a Latin quiz. What importance do you
attach to Nat's study of Latin poetry in the years after his college
career is over?

Taylor: I felt it was an indication of his having a more spiritual
nature which he'd never developed. He was reaching out for something other than the business and practical world he lived in and his
family was associated with.

Touchstone: Why Latin?

Taylor: I chose it because I was taking a Latin course myself at that
age. The story is based on an actual event: an automobile accident I
had in exactly the same spot—also, it is the world I grew up in. There
is a suggestion of the world Nat's grandfathers and great-grandfathers
knew, a world of classically-educated planters.

> . . . the road crossed the streetcar tracks and entered a densely wooded
> area which is actually the last surviving bit of the primeval forest that once
> grew right up to the bluffs of the Mississippi . . . Some of them surely may
> have been mature trees when Hernando de Soto passed this way . . . I
> saw a truck approaching on the wrong side of the icy road. . . . When he
> was within about seventy-five feet of us, Lee Ann said, "Pull off the road,
> Nat!" . . .

Touchstone: In your description of the old forest—into which
"demimondame" Lee Ann Deehart disappears—you speak of those
pioneer women who ran off to the woods, some living with the
Indians, others simply "disappearing" as does Robert Frost's Hill
Wife.

Taylor: I had in mind certain people who simply walked out,
disappeared. I know of one woman—they found her car and clothes
on the banks of the Mississippi. Assumption was that she committed
suicide. Another case: I had a cousin that just disappeared one day

and set his house on fire so his wife could collect insurance. He was never found in his whole life.

Touchstone: To what extent is the seasonal setting important? I find it interesting that this action occurs in early December, before Nat's marriage, before Christmas.

Taylor: I don't know whether I have any ideas on that or not—I don't think I do. The war—remember this is 1937—is there looming, is going to open up and change everything. About the season, I really didn't have any symbolic notions about it.

Touchstone: The men of this story assume a paternalistic attitude toward these young women of the demi-monde.

Taylor: Yes, I was trying to suggest the authority that certain men felt as a class responsibility—a real authority, a genuine responsibility. This was a much more homogeneous society. These men felt they were fathers to all these young women. Also, though the world was changing, they were still behaving as their fathers had behaved.

Touchstone: Of course, it is Nat's fiancee Caroline, not the men at all, who brings Lee Ann out of hiding.

> The only power I had to save myself was to save you Nat, and to save you by rescuing Lee Ann Deehart. It always came to that, and comes to that still. Don't you see, it was a question of how very much I had to lose and how little power I had to save myself. Because I had not set myself free the way those other girls have.
>
> Caroline Braxley, Nat's fiancee.

Taylor: Caroline had to save Nat for herself. If Lee Ann never came back, the marriage would have been impossible. It had to be made clear that no harm had come to Lee Ann.

There is the bond Caroline feels between Lee Ann and herself as a woman. I had this idea when writing—this theme emerging in my mind. The form I took rose from discovering my scene and all the possiblities in it. When I fix on a theme, I really amuse myself with it. I was thinking about the different kinds of women.

Touchstone: I know it's terribly unfair to ask an author these questions about conscious and unconscious design.

Taylor: You don't ever honestly set out to do all you do. I didn't set out to prove a point but to tell a story. I sometimes find myself getting off on a theme which is not in my experience, then I try to swing it back.

Touchstone: You find yourself repeating the same sort of stories, then.

Taylor: I have a horror of formulas. One time when I was under contract to *The New Yorker,* they called and said if I'd turn in another story before the month was up, my contract percentage would rise from 15% to 25%; that meant a great deal of money. I went over to the college and sat down and wrote a story—it has been 25 years and I would never publish that story anywhere else. I felt bad about it—Oh, God, I am becoming a *New Yorker* writer. I wrote a number of stories about old women. When I wrote "Miss Lenora When Last Seen," that was the last—the end of those stories.

Touchstone: Back to "The Old Forest." Though it's Caroline's story, Lee Ann is also transformed by her moment in the old forest; in many ways, she emerges domesticated.

Taylor: She comes to terms with things. It all took place literally right here. There was the battle to save the trees in Overton Park—it made me think about those woods—what it is like in the trees— urban and yet primitive.

Touchstone: The way Memphis seems to preserve two worlds has always fascinated me.

Taylor: When Steve Ross was selecting the house he was going to film, he selected a house for [Caroline]—79 Morningside Park. Without any suggestion from me. This was the house where I lived as a boy; my sister was married in that house. I think this shows how much he has really sensed the spirit of this story. In the scene where the police interview the girl on the loading platform, he filmed exactly the same warehouse I had in mind when writing—the Orgill Brothers Warehouse. Both of these instances make it hard for me to be objective about this.

I've just today had a letter from my publisher at Doubleday; they are terribly excited about the film.

Touchstone: You have a new collection coming out.

Taylor: Yes, *The Old Forest and Other Stories.* It contains two stories that have never been collected before, "The Old Forest" and "The Gift of the Prodigal."

Touchstone: Your work remains what might be called "my-thopoetic," then.

Taylor: Yes. My view of Tennessee may be childish—as though that small area contained the whole world in it. It is very interesting to go back to Memphis and to see how much it is still as it was—a little walled city or town within the City. I've enjoyed talking about this; I'm not very good at it. Never know what course to pursue.

PW Interviews: Peter Taylor
Wendy Smith/1985

From *Publishers Weekly*, 18 January 1985, 77–78. Reprinted
with the permission of *Publishers Weekly* and Wendy Smith.

The South has traditionally been one of America's more gothic
literary landscapes: suffering and violence grow in abundance there,
at least in writer's imaginations, and Southern prose is usually as
luxuriant as the foliage. For more than 40 years, however, Peter
Taylor has cast a cool, classical eye on his native territory, delineating
changes in its socio-economic structure and dissecting its inhabitants'
passions in elegant, measured language more reminiscent of Henry
James than William Faulkner.

Yet Taylor's work is as distinctively Southern as he is. *The Old
Forest and Other Stories* (Dial/Doubleday, Fiction Forecasts, Dec. 21)
collects 12 previously published and two recently written short stories
delving into the lives of the people among whom Taylor grew up:
wealthy, aristocratic Southerners whose families picked themselves
up after the debacle of the Civil War, left the plantations and moved
into the South's growing cities to become lawyers, doctors, cotton
brokers—a new professional class whose code of behavior was still
firmly rooted in antebellum moral values.

It's the effect of this external reality on the private concerns of his
characters that interests Taylor, whose own life has been at once
deeply rooted in the South and also detached from it by the
exigencies of first his father's and then his own career. Growing up all
over the South and Midwest, spending every summer in the Tennessee mountains, he now lives in Charlottesville, Va., near the
university where he taught for many years. The Taylors' handsome,
gray clapboard house is in the colonial style, not an antebellum
mansion by any means, but Southern in mood nonetheless. The
library in which he chats with *PW* contains an almost Victorian
profusion of furniture (including a red settee that was a gift from the
writer Jean Stafford, a lifelong friend) and books (complete sets of

Henry James and Anthony Trollope jostle short story collections by
Tolstoy and Chekhov, with the works of Faulkner and other Southern
writers also prominent).

The library also displays several paintings, one of which is a full-
size portrait of Taylor's great-grandfather. Its companion, a painting of
the author's great-grandmother and her children, hangs in the adjoining room. "Very Tennessee, don't you think?" remarks their de-
scendent, whose attitude is affectionate but hardly respectful and
whose own accent is also "very Tennessee." A handsome man in his
late 60s, with a strongly lined face framed by a shock of white hair,
Taylor wears both his age and his aristocratic heritage lightly. Unlike
many modern writers, he remains deeply connected to his family and
its history, but he views both with an amused detachment that
suggests a man at peace with his past.

Taylor's wife, the poet Eleanor Ross Taylor, is at home working
today, but although her husband speaks with her briefly in another
room, she does not appear to greet his visitor. "She's in her
bathrobe," Taylor explains. "We both love to work in our pajamas!
We write in the morning and try not to see each other before lunch at
2 o'clock, because if we do, if we meet and start talking, then before
we know it, the day's already gone. She works upstairs, and I work
just underneath this room—we have a basement that opens out on
the garden—so that we can't hear each other's typewriters. I find it
depressing to hear somebody else's when mine won't go!"

Although Taylor is essentially a short story writer, most of his work
begins as verse. "I write nearly everything that way," he says. "I like it
because you get more emphasis on the groups of words and the
language and the rhythms. I can't sustain it very long, but I try to
finish a story in verse, then go back and put it into prose. I began
writing that way as an effort to compress; in a story you have very
limited space, so every sentence has to do more. I have a theory that
a story ought to do as much as a novel, and a poem ought to do as
much as a story—in fact, if a poem doesn't do a great deal more with
its language, with the form, then it's not as good as a story."

His method is certainly unusual, but given his history it's not
surprising that Taylor should work in verse. Not only is he married to
a poet, but at Vanderbilt University and Kenyon College in the late
1930s he studied with the influential Southern poets Allen Tate and

John Crowe Ransom. In that same period, he also met two contemporaries who would become his lifelong friends: poets Robert Lowell and Randall Jarrell. "It was wonderful, and it certainly had a great deal to do with my going on in writing," says Taylor. "To come at that age into a group of people who were very highbrow, very serious and articulate about writing. You learn so much from your peers; I always tell my students that. I learned a lot from Tate and Ransom, but more from Lowell and Jarrell."

Jarrell, who was four years older than Taylor, was a formidable critic. "Kenyon was his first teaching job, I think," says Taylor, "and we were all sort of scared of him. If he didn't like what you wrote, he would get furious at you. One time, when he and I were both living in a little town in Italy, I passed him on the street, and he wouldn't speak to me. I saw his wife later and said, 'Well, what in the world?' and she answered, 'Well, he doesn't like that new story of yours.' He would do the same thing to Lowell. The first thing was, you were his friend, but there was this *other* you that had done this awful thing! But he'd get over it, and later he might even come to like the piece. This is often true of your friends: if you change and begin writing something rather different from what you'd done before, they don't always want you to, because they liked what you'd been doing. I know when Lowell broke from his formal verse and began to write more freely, I was very critical—but I was wrong. He needed to break out and deal with his experience more directly."

Taylor was Lowell's close friend for nearly 40 years (the poet died in 1977), and when he speaks of their relationship his tone is warm. "We never had any real quarrel," he says. "He was a wonderful friend; he could make you feel good about anything. One of the problems with Ian Hamilton's biography, although I thought it was good in many ways, was that it didn't give any impression of the other side of him. He had the most marvelous sense of humor; he was the gentlest person and the most loyal of friends. He was lots of fun to be with, just to talk to; he would call, and we would talk on the telephone for hours. Our wives used to say that we liked each other's jokes so much that we would sit up telling stories we'd heard a dozen times before, and we would just roar with laughter!

"Lowell had a tremendous influence on me when I was beginning to write," Taylor continues. "For example, all through college I took

Latin and had a great respect for classical literature—not a profound
knowledge, but respect and an acquaintance with it. I had always
wanted to be a fiction writer, but I just wrote stories wildly without
much form or much reference to the formal history of literature. His
concern with poetry from Homer to William Carlos Williams, his
need to have it all in place, to understand it and incorporate what he
needed in his own work, made me try to read fiction more with a
view to its form than I would have otherwise. Of course, poets are
often more articulate about things and more concerned with tradition.
He made me more scholarly than I would have been otherwise; I
might just have read contemporary material, as most young writers
do."

The deep seriousness and reverence for tradition that Lowell
imparted to him are reflected in Taylor's fairly classical beliefs about
what fiction should do. "My feeling is that stories ought to be about
something that's over and done with, so you can judge it properly,"
he says. "You can't really trust what writers say about their work, but
it seems to me that what I'm trying to do in my stories is to look at
the characters from several points of view, to make sure that I'm at a
distance so that I can discover what this character's like and how to
look at it. And so I felt that during integration, for example, I couldn't
really write about it." (Taylor's stories, in fact, are virtually all set
before 1954.)

This doesn't mean that Taylor's fiction won't engage issues or make
moral judgements. "I think writing fiction is a cognitive instrument,"
he says. "You learn what you really think from what you write. My
parents were great storytellers, and so were our (black) servants; they
were all part of that Southern oral tradition. As a young writer
aspiring to be an artist, I just had to do something with those
stories—they were so marvelous. My parents didn't have any idea of
moral or intellectual judgment; a story was just a funny story or a sad
story to them. But as I put them down on paper, I began to see that
in all these fine old Southern stories blacks were getting the short end
from women, who were getting the short end from men. I didn't
know what they meant until I wrote them."

Taylor's parents weren't always happy about his use of old family
tales in his fiction. "My father once even threatened my physically
because of a story that came out in the *New Yorker* about my great-

aunt," he remembers. "It wasn't really about her, but it used an
incident from her life. People don't understand that in fiction you're
just using them for character and detail; they're not concerned with
the basic ideas of the story. You have to use the details, just as you
use colors in a painting, but what's important is the interplay, the
contrast of people's lives with the decline of society, or the deterioration of the family. The real poetry emerges in the coincidence
between the context and the character, as in Chekhov's stories: the
estate is going to pieces, the whole order is falling apart, and the
characters are the same—there's no satisfaction, nothing's working,
and that all makes sense. In Ibsen too: the gloom of Scandinavia and
the characters' gloom do something to each other; they interpret each
other, make you believe in them, like rhyme and meter in poetry."

In Taylor's own stories, the characters' personal preoccupations and
behavior do indeed reflect the larger nature of the South, but in a
subtle, unmythical way that may account for his curious lack of fame:
America seems to prefer its Southern writers to be more flamboyant.
"It's partly temperament," says Taylor of his restrained approach.
"Also, although I admire all these mythical writers about the South
tremendously—I'm just a slave to Faulkner; I think he's wonderful,
and Eudora Welty and Katherine Anne Porter—I thought it was time
to try something else." As for his admirers' loudly expressed belief
that he deserves to be better known—"I don't write for that," he says
simply. "I've always had a lot of appreciative literary friends, and
maybe that meant more to me than it should have, but it's all chance
whether or not you become well known in your generation. My
concern is with how good what I write is and with the opinion of my
peers."

Taylor has let the outside world influence him to the extent of
writing his third novel recently, (His first, A Woman of Means, was
published in 1954 and reissued last year by Frederic C. Beil; a
second was destroyed by Taylor in the 1960s when he decided it was
unsatisfactory.). "It used to infuriate me, the attitude that you wrote
stories until you were good enough to write a novel," he says. "I
much prefer reading stories: I like James's stories better than his
novels, and Faulkner's, and I think D. H. Lawrence's stories are much
better than his novels. But people always pressure you, and it does
seem like a challenge—the scope of it. So I've just completed a

second draft, and it needs about one more. It may not be any good, but I have written it, by George. I wanted to see if I could write a novel."

Work seems to get done faster now that he's no longer teaching full time, Taylor finds. "I guess it kept me from writing more than I realized," he says, "but it taught me a great deal too. I think teaching's been good for me: I'm a very gregarious person, I like to be with people, and it's also made me more articulate. I wanted to do something to support my family and not feel they were interfering with my writing. So many writers have to just turn it out, and it shouldn't be that sort of thing. The writers I knew—and that's how I feel too—thought that you write out of compulsion, because there's a need to tell a story or to write a poem; you don't write because you've go to have another book out this year. Professionalism gets very near commercialism. Now, some writers, like F. Scott Fitzgerald, just have to be in the mainstream, and that's right for them, so I wouldn't want to make rules about it. But I think, generally speaking, people do better if they have another profession and don't depend on their writing to make a living. Because if you do, you've got to please the public: you try to fit your writing to their taste instead of forming the taste. Most good writers—and by good writers, I mean really good ones, like Proust or Lowell—didn't answer the demands of an audience; they created a whole new one. And that's what you should aspire to."

Symbols and Themes Mature into Plots

Caryn James/1985

From *The New York Times Book Review*, 17 February 1985, 26. © 1985 by The New York Times Company. Reprinted by permission.

A photograph taken in 1941—the year the earliest of the works collected in Peter Taylor's *The Old Forest and Other Stories* appeared—shows the 22-year-old author with Robert Lowell and Jean Stafford, who became his lifetime friends. Mr. Taylor's gentle Southern voice becomes louder, laughing, when reminded of it. He is on the phone in Gainesville, Fla., but instantly recognizes the photograph described. "That's the funniest picture. Jean always said she looked like a keeper at some institution and we looked like two inmates. I think that's true, but I cherish that picture."

His conversation is cordial, free of glib replies, as he recalls student days with Lowell at Kenyon College and Louisiana State University. Those times still influence his stories, which often take the shapes of poems or plays. "I was a poet first. I studied with John Crowe Ransom, Allen Tate and Cleanth Brooks. The formalists influenced me. I think stories and plays are both dramatic forms; compression is everything." He also discerns changes in his work. "When I was very young, if someone mentioned plot I thought they were so vulgar and crass. I have stories that are buried, I hope forever, in little magazines, and they're just full of symbols and themes. In later years, I've gotten more interested in plot." That interest is crucial to his novel-in-progress, which began as a story. "I started thinking about my father, then about other people I knew; there was enough interplay between the stories to make a novel. It's a comedy about a rich old man whose children try to prevent his remarrying, and it ranges back over their earlier lives. It's about revenge upon and forgiveness of parents. Maturity, in a way, is forgiving your parents." Mr. Taylor accepts maturity with grace. Retired from the University of Virginia, he says, "My best friends used to be my former teachers. Now I'm so old they're my former students."

66

A Conversation with Peter Taylor

J. William Broadway/1985

From *The Chattahoochee Review*, 6 (Fall 1985), 17–44, 61– 75. Reprinted by permission.

Nearly four decades after the publication of his first book, Peter Hillsman Taylor finally is gaining the widespread recognition he deserves. Among a limited number of readers, respect has never been lacking for his simply told, complex stories about the urban South.

"I was Peter's first college English teacher," Allen Tate once wrote, "but I found I could not teach him anything, so I asked him to leave the class after about two weeks. The simple truth is that he did not need to know anything I could teach him. He had a perfection of style at the age of 18 that I envied."

From the time he entered Tate's class at Southwestern in Memphis through periods of study with John Crowe Ransom at Vanderbilt and Kenyon and in the years thereafter, Taylor established a circle of friends who offered the encouragement and support he needed to develop his already appreciable skills. This group included his closest compatriots Robert Lowell and Randall Jarrell and other renowned writers such as Robert Penn Warren, Cleanth Brooks, Andrew Lytle, Jean Stafford, Eudora Welty, and Katherine Anne Porter.

Taylor's first story appeared in the March 1937 issue of the short-lived *River* magazine. His most prodigious output occurred in the two decades following the 1948 publication of his first collection, *A Long Fourth and Other Stories*, which included a laudatory introduction by Warren. Stories in the old *Southern Review, Kenyon Review, Sewanee Review, Shenandoah,* and—most importantly—in the *New Yorker* established his reputation among the literati as a writer of the first rank.

Despite this exposure and the publication of seven short-story collections, one novella, and a group of dramatic pieces, Taylor's name has failed to become a familiar one. While many critics attribute his lack of popular readership to his not having published a major novel, the

truth probably lies more with his own reluctance to pro-
mote himself and his works.

The publication of *The Old Forest and Other Stories* on
February 8, 1986, initiated a surge of publicity that has
brought Taylor thousands of new admirers. While only
authorizing a small first printing of 6,000 copies, Dial
Press/Doubleday barraged the media with promotional
materials and sponsored showings of the movie *The Old
Forest,* produced and directed by Steven Ross of
Memphis State University.

The Old Forest had a large review distribution around
the country in newspapers, national news magazines, and
literary magazines and journals. The short-story collection is in its fifth printing with a total of 20,000 copies, and
Ballantine Books has purchased the rights to publish the
work in paperback next spring.

The success of *The Old Forest* proved to be the catalyst
for the paperback publication of two other works, both
scheduled for early 1986: Taylor's short novel, *A Woman
of Means,* by Avon for its Southern Writers Series, and
the reissue of *The Collected Stories* by Penguin, which
bought the softcover rights from Farrar Straus, for its
Contemporary American Fiction series. Frederic Beil,
who brought out a fine limited edition reprint of *A
Woman of Means* in 1983, will publish next year a hard-
cover revision of *A Stand in the Mountains,* a play.

While not an aggressive self-promoter, Peter Taylor
graciously accepted phone call after phone call and interview after interview following the publication of *The Old
Forest.* This conversation took place on February 15 in
Gainesville, Florida, at the winter home Taylor shares
with his wife, poet Eleanor Ross Taylor.

The three-bedroom home, located in the northeast
historic district of the city, at first appeared incongruous
with the personalities of avowed "fanciers of old houses."
The clapboard exterior of the 50-year-old, low-lying cinderblock structure had been replaced with artificial stucco
when the house was remodeled in 1984, the trim painted
brown, and oversized numbers posted near the front
door.

Other features seemed more appropriate. The large lot
was bordered by a creek and had plenty of sun-filled
garden areas framed by 200-year-old oak trees draped
with Spanish moss and ferns. Inside, rustic pieces infused
the simple living space with touches of the past: antique

kitchen safes, a small round mahogany table with ladder-back chairs, a leather-covered end table, a carved wood duck lamp, and wooden benches more than a century old.

Wearing his favorite red-and-white-striped oxford cloth shirt and tweed jacket, Taylor received me in his inimitably charming manner. He spoke animatedly on virtually any topic raised, smiling and laughing frequently and talking, always, in a gently assertive voice.

Neither of us, I suspect, had any idea the conversation would stretch into five hours and diminish only as dusk fell around the huge oaks and filled the room with soft evening light. The air was one of transcendence as past and present merged, and the ghosts of Jarrell, Lowell, Tate, and Ransom loomed larger with the passing hours. For a brief period the tables were turned, and Peter Taylor became the seen and not the seer.

Broadway: You've just gotten back from New York and the publication party for *The Old Forest and Other Stories.* How do you feel about all the activities surrounding the book?

Taylor: I'll tell you exactly. Until the first of March I'm part of publishing. I'm going out and doing everything they ask me to do. I'm giving readings, and they made a film of the title story. But after the first of March I'm *my* animal again. We live a very private life.

Broadway: What are they planning to do with the film?

Taylor: Oh, it's for public television. I don't know anything about filmmaking. But I learned a lot. I went and watched (producer/director) Steve Ross finish the editing. He's a brilliant young man who has a very good literary sense as well as a cinematic sense. He came to me three times to talk about the film and told me what he thought the story was about and what he was doing with it. And I was taken by his perceptiveness. I think in the end he is completely faithful to the story. The only other experience that I had with television films was a commercial thing, so it wasn't at all the same.

Broadway: I read somewhere about the coincidence of his picking a house you once lived in as the house of Caroline Braxley in the film.

Taylor: I didn't live there very long. It was a house I lived in in my teens. It was just the purest chance. He called me and said, "I've found the house for Caroline." He said it was in Morningside Park. And I said, "What number?" And he said "79" and I said, "I don't believe it. That's the house we lived in back in the '30s."

Broadway: And when you saw it on the screen?

Taylor: It was just uncanny. The first time—I've seen it twice now in New York—the first time I just couldn't watch it. I could hardly think about the story because there was the house. The house one of my sisters was married in, the stairs she was married on. When I told her, she just screamed with delight.

Broadway: Your wife's maiden name is Ross. Does Steve Ross happen to be related?

Taylor: No, no. There's no connection at all. He had never been south of the Mason Dixon Line until this. And he was just amazed by Memphis. How everybody's kin to each other and knew each other and what continuity there is there in society. And has been for a long time. My wife was a Ross, of course. And her brothers are both marvelous.

Broadway: Aren't they called "the writing Rosses?"

Taylor: Yes. The "writing Rosses of North Carolina." That refers to my wife and her two brothers James and Fred. And her sister also is publishing short stories now in the best magazines. Jean Ross Justice. Her husband is the one who teaches poetry. They're all writers. They're very unlike my family. My family is not given to literature.

Broadway: How many people were in your family?

Taylor: Four children. I was the youngest. My parents are both dead now, of course. I have a sister at Johns Island, Florida, near Vero Beach. My other sister is dead, and my brother lives in San Antonio.

Broadway: Where are your children now, Katie and Peter?

Taylor: My daughter has a farm and raises cattle in Orange County near Chapel Hill. And my son is in Washington. He has begun publishing poems for magazines and works at the Kennedy Center's performing arts library. He went to the Iowa Writers Workshop and got a degree. But he got chosen for this job in Washington. And he loves Washington. Washington is a nice place to live now if you're young. More than it was when I came along. There's a lot more life there.

Broadway: Where is Peter publishing?

Taylor: Mainly in little magazines. He has a poem in the new issue of *Shenandoah.* And my daughter writes fiction and she's had a few stories around in the little quarterlies. But they are both determined not to be known because their parents are writers. My son used to be known as Peter Taylor. His name is Peter Ross Taylor, but he writes as Ross Taylor.

I believe very much in young writers—I preach it to my students and I guess I have to my children, too—that young writers begin to write in the little magazines. Little magazines make more serious literary judgments about the work of a young writer, and they don't get into the rat race of trying to publish in the slicks, the big time. I think it's much better for people if they want to develop their own way of writing.

Broadway: Is that basically the way you did it?

Taylor: That's the way I did it, and maybe that's why I believe in the idea. When I came along everybody did that, and they still do to some extent. People begin with those magazines because they really select people more than the big magazines do. They're interested in discovering people. They don't have the money to buy the big writers, the famous ones. So they can encourage young writers and they can get good writers that way. So it's a much better opportunity for young writers.

A big magazine, a slick magazine, will do some first writers, but they like names. Except in the *New Yorker,* I don't think they do. Most would rather print a bad story— not that he writes bad stories— say by Saul Bellow than a good story by John Jones, who has never published anything. They want to sell magazines.

Yet you want the big magazines to go on because they are a good support to literature; they help good writers make a living.

Broadway: How do you convince young writers they will get the big break if they start out with the little magazines?

Taylor: My logic, or at least my rationalization, is that what happens to you in little magazines—and I've seen it happen to myself and many others—is that Best Short Stories and the O. Henry collection often pick storiess from those little magazines. They can't pick all the stories from *Esquire, Playboy, New Yorker* and *Mademoiselle.* They like to think they are high, and they are high.

They are making literary judgments. They will always pick some stories, say, from *Shenandoah* or other literary magazines—*Partisan Review, Sewanee Review, Kenyon Review* or whatever. And the newer ones. So it seems to me that's the sensible way.

It's a hard row to hoe any way you go, much harder now than it used to be. For one thing, there are so many more people writing and there are fewer serious, good magazines. You get competition and there is almost a blurring, the way there is in music, between the high brow and the middle brow and the low brow. You don't get the distinctions like you once did.

It used to be the *Kenyon Review* and the *Partisan Review* and the *Southern Review,* the old *Southern Review,* the *Virginia Quarterly Review* and the *Sewanee Review*—everybody who was a serious reader of fiction and poetry read those magazines. And you could count on being seen there if you were printed. One thing you used to find—and I suppose still do—as soon as you published in one of those magazines, you got a letter from a publisher saying "Do you have a novel?" They watched them.

Though there is nothing morally wrong in publishing right away in a *Redbook* or something, I don't think they are so apt to select the original, fresh sort of writer. They want to print something that's in fashion already. More or less they have to. They are in the business. And these little magazines want to discover new, fresh, different writers.

Broadway: But you say the distinctions are blurring now?

Taylor: What I mean is the big magazines try to reach out and get these young writers. There is so much effort now to corrupt them. Not corrupt them in a literal sense but to lead them away, to give them quick success. I'm not really casting aspersions on them. I don't blame them. But the little magazines don't have the authority. There are so many little magazines now. They begin and stop and maybe that's good that they do. For a number of years we had sort of standard, major quarterlies we published in.

Broadway: So although there are more of the little magazines, there aren't as many that are recognized as the place to get started?

Taylor: That's precisely right. It used to be that if you were going to print, you could do it, say, in the *Partisan Review* or the *Southern Review,* which were opposite in the '30s. The *Southern Review* was the Agrarian magazine, more politically conservative. Robert Penn Warren, John Crowe Ransom, Cleanth Brooks, all those people. And the *Partisan Review* was run by New York left-wing writers. But as a matter of fact, they printed a good many of the same writers because they were making literary judgments. They didn't choose a story because of its political slant at all.

Of course the *New Yorker* has always had a certain standing of its own. And you know if you're printed in the *New Yorker*, you know you're going to get a large readership, too. It pays so much more than any other magazine and its standards are so much more real. I think it is a true literary magazine in the sense that its editors don't select the stories or the articles or the poetry according to the name.

Broadway: What was the writing environment when you were starting out?

Taylor: I must admit I was very lucky when I was young. I came along when there were a lot of good writers in the South—living in the South, not just from the South. And of course Warren and Brooks and Tate and Ransom and Lytle all lived in Tennessee. And Katherine Anne Porter. They were accessible. I would go to them and they would read my work, and if they liked your work it was a great satisfaction. If your *friends* liked your work. If you weren't famous or rich but still you had a circle of literary people who appreciated your work. That was really much more important to you than the other. And that's always been true for me.

Broadway: What was the first story you published in the *New Yorker?*

Taylor: In the *New Yorker* I think it's called "Middle Age." I change the name of my stories and then I can't always remember which one I published it under. Anyway, that was after the war and after the publication of my first collection. *A Long Fourth and Other Stories,* in 1948. But I'd published before the war stories in the *Southern Review* and the Partisan Review and in the *New Republic.*

The *New Yorker* had turned down several of my stories. Then they wrote me about a story that they'd read and they wanted me to send them something. Well, I had already sent them the very story they wrote me about before I sent it to the little magazine. So I was irked. I was a long-haired youngster. And so I waited awhile and then I sent them a story. It was a couple of years later and I was *amazed* when

they said that they'd accepted it. I'll never forget. After I published
that one in the *New Yorker*, they published a good many.

Broadway: And you did this all on your own without an agent?

Taylor: I never had much luck with agents. I have an agent now,
but I don't know why I do. If you're a very prolific writer and have a
lot of business dealings—selling novels to the movies—you need a
business manager. Otherwise, I don't think they are of much great
use to a young writer. Except they help them get a larger advance
from the publisher. But then in the end a larger advance is sort of a
vanity. You have to pay it back if your book makes any money. So I
suppose they're useful that way.

But I know how I was when I worked in a publishing house. I was
in New York and had a job at Henry Holt. I was just a reader, very
low on the totem pole. Letters would come from an agent saying,
"Here is a young writer that we think deserves a chance. It's the best
young writer that's come along." I was always reading it with the
attitude of "I'll see whether that's so or not." But if it just came from
the young writer saying humbly, "Won't you read my work?" I was
much more likely than not to read it.

Broadway: This attitude you're expressing about agents, New
York publishing houses and so forth—do you think it may have hurt
you as far as your reputation? No one seems to be able to put a
finger on why you are not better known.

Taylor: I don't know. I have a review somebody sent me the other
day that expresses my view, my idea about it. It's a review of *The Old
Forest* written by a young writer I know in Washington (Stephen
Goodwin, "One Writer Who Can See the Forest and the Trees,"
Washington Weekly, Feb. 15, 1985). It begins:

"Let me describe an ideal literary career. The writer has a sense of
the work cut out for him at an early age. He is eager to get going. At
college he makes friends—lifelong friends, as it turns out—with some
of the best writers of his generation. When he begins to publish short
stories, it is clear he has already found his subject matter, and his own
unmistakable voice.

"His work appears first in the prestigious literary magazines, later
the *New Yorker*, giving him as large an audience as a short story
writer could wish for. He has the most exacting readers, those friends
of his—poets Randall Jarrell and Robert Lowell—respond at length,

in detail and with delight to his fiction. Honors come his way, and he steadily extends and fulfills his gifts. Forty years after he began he is still writing stories fresh as bread . . . This writer, of course, is Peter Taylor."

He's saying that the kind of reputation, the kind of career I've had is in a sense more satisfying than other kinds. Because I have always had very highbrow literary friends who were very critical and yet very responsive and made a good life. And I wrote for myself and I wrote what I wanted to write.

I think it's a very spirited and witty piece. And it's saying the reverse thing of my not being well known. He quotes me as saying that I'm happy to be the best known unknown writer." (Laughs.)

Broadway: So it doesn't bother you . . .

Taylor: If you're a serious writer, you want to be able to do your work and have warm response to it by intelligent readers and not try to be a movie star, not try to be a culture hero. That's why I've never worried about having agents or living in New York. I don't think it was the road for me. That's just my temperament, I guess. But then the older writers I knew were that way. John Crowe Ransom was a great friend and teacher of mine, and he lived a very quiet life and was much respected. Of course, he was not a famous writer in the sense that Ezra Pound was.

Broadway: We talked earlier about how your characters almost always come to some point of recognition and how similar feelings appear in the stories of James Joyce in the form of "epiphanies." Thinking of Joyce brings another comparison to mind. While you have experienced relative anonymity among the general public, Joyce was a person who really promoted himself. It was extraordinary the way he went about it. He badgered publishers, the public, the press, everybody.

Taylor: Oh, he did. And he was famous as a writer before he ever published a line. I know he was a remarkable person, but he must have been an impressive person to have been able to do that. Writers can be entirely different, as different as lawyers and doctors, I try to tell young writers that just because one writer is one way they don't have to be the same way.

I've even seen writers who thought you had to be a drunkard. And I had one writer tell me once—a writer who was a homosexual—that you really couldn't be a writer if you weren't a homosexual. (Laughs.) I mean people would develop that sort of attitude because they had certain feelings and liked to live a certain way. It has *nothing* to do with it. Writers are totally different.

And a writer can be a terribly fraudulent person in some ways and a liar and yet be a very good writer when you get right down to it. The terrible faults that they discover in writers after they're dead. You know, how they've done about Frost and Hemingway. What do they expect? Writers are just other men.

It's never been a great matter of interest to me this business, because I've always been well known enough. And to be accepted among my peers. It's always been funny to me from various times people would say to me about some other writer, "He published this novel and he didn't have to write any short stories or anything." And that always offended me, because I don't think that writing short stories is the same thing as writing a novel. And you don't write short stories just so you can learn how to write a novel. At least I didn't. I wrote stories because it was a form that suited me.

Broadway: Do you think some people use short story writing as an experiment just to develop style?

Taylor: Well, people think that's what it is. But if you judge short fiction that way, you'd have to judge lyric poetry the same way, too. And everybody knows that isn't right. A short, lyric poem—Milton's, Shakespeare's, Browning's, Ransom's—is a more concentrated, compressed, intense use of the language.

I think a short story must be relatively so to a novel. That you must do more in ten pages than you do in ten pages of a novel. That you must be able to suggest a whole world, as Chekhov does. That in a novel you really expose the world. You develop it. A poem suggests even more; there are always implications. I don't say these are absolute truths because you can take some poems, some stories that are good stories, that don't have much intensity or compression. But the great ones do.

Broadway: Do you find that critics who read your works make too much of the implications, the suggestions?

Taylor: Someone sent me an article from a magazine called the *Southern Partisan* (John Douglas Minyard, "Which Southern Writers are Southern Writers?" Summer 1984). It's a well-written article, but

I'm not sure that I agree with it. It says that I'm Virgilian and Jarrell is
a Platonist and it goes into all those philosophical ideas behind Virgil,
Plato and Socrates. But you get these various articles, and they aren't
what you meant. That's not what I had in mind.

On the other hand, people will sometimes write about my work,
and I will realize things about it that I hadn't thought of before. A
friend of mine teaching in Florida about fifteen years ago sent me a
group of papers that his students had written. And this is the sort of
attention I've had always. I've had colleges, people reading my
stories in colleges, being in anthologies.

And he sent me an analysis of "The Walled Garden," interpreting
it—well, they all interpreted it—as a Freudian story. As I read their
papers I began to think, "Well, you know, that didn't occur to me
while I was writing it, but in a way that's why it works as well as it
does." I think it's often true for writers. And you will find a Roman
Catholic critic who will like the same story as a Freudian critic and
they will have their different literary principles they're working with. I
suppose there are certain universals in criticism.

Broadway: You are working on a novel now. Is that correct?

Taylor: I am, simply because it got out of hand. It's a story that got
out of hand. And that's what a novel is for me. I've written one, two
others as a matter of fact. I tore up one of them and I burned it
because I thought it was boring. I never got the life into it somehow. I
never had the second inspiration you have to have.

But that's what a novel is for me, and the themes are such that it
requires more space to present it in. I can't really define it, except that
I do think that a novel allows for digressions. And the reader actually
wants that. For instance, we read Trollope all the time. This one (on
the end table) is called *Can You Forgive Her?* Well, Trollope just goes
off on little essays about fox hunting and anything that comes along
in a novel. And it's fun to read that way. But that's not what a lyric
poem does. You want a certain intensity and seriousness, a unity.
You can't afford not to in a lyric poem or short story.

I just read a long review in *The New York Times Book Review*
(Robert Towers, "A Master of the Miniature Novel," Feb. 17, 1985).
Have you seen it?

Broadway: Yes, I have.

Taylor: It speaks of my stories as being miniature novels. Well, in a sense they are. I thought of them that way to some extent, of suggesting a whole world. But there are other people who have done that before. I got some ideas of doing that from some Thomas Mann stories and Tolstoy's short novels. When you remember them you think of them as much longer than they are because they suggest worlds.

There were several things in the review I couldn't understand. Like comparing me to writers like John O'Hara and Irwin Shaw. In the first place, they're a totally different generation—he's wrong about my being in that generation. And my stories aren't nearly as much concerned with class matters as he seems to think.

Broadway: Do you have conscious intentions when you sit down to write a story?

Taylor: It's very hard to talk about your own fiction this way. Because it's so easy to say in retrospect what you meant to do. Actually, my notion of writing a story is that you have a story that occurs to you and as you write it, you learn what that story means to you. I don't have ideas about what life is and then go and find myself a story to illustrate it.

I'm a person who likes to tell stories and in the course of telling them . . . Well, for instance, early in writing I realized that many of the stories I knew while growing up were about Southern blacks and whites living together. And about the Southern scene. And they were supposed to be funny stories or sad stories. In fact, my mother and father and other family members were telling stories, and I had this compulsion to write.

And as I wrote those stories, I began to see that the blacks were often getting the short end from the whites. And the women were getting the short end from the men. I didn't have any strong feelings that I was going to go out and improve the world. I wanted to write those stories. And so as I told them, what I thought came out, to my own surprise sometimes. James said about writing fiction that a profound mind can only produce a profound story, and a shallow mind will produce a shallow story. There's nothing you can do about that if you're a writer.

Broadway: Many people have pointed out a certain, if you will, effeminate manner or element to your stories. How do you know so much about women and what they think and how they act?

Taylor: For one thing, I grew up in an old Southern family with lots of old aunts and cousins. My father was a lawyer who looked after a lot of the spinsters and widows in the family. And they were always around us. There were men, too, but I think the impulse in writing is to make a leap toward understanding what other people unlike yourself are like.

Often people take my stories that have a male narrator whose history seems to be like my background and think it's me. And it's not. I seldom have a narrator that I mean for the reader to accept literally all the way through the story. They are only suggestions. I'm thinking of somebody else, my brother or my friends. I've had all of them, even my father, *blast* me for my stories. "If you'd been home when that last story came out, I'd have knocked you down." (Laughs.) I was trying to write about his best friend. But he didn't recognize that.

It's a leap of the imagination and that's what fiction should be about. That's the way it's constructed to the writer. You try to understand how the world is from other points of view. James does it often. Good writers have always done it. But I did write a lot about women, and in a way it was trying to understand them and trying to take the opposite view from the one I would naturally take.

I'll give you another example. I wrote a story called "The Spinster's Tale" about an old lady telling stories of when she was young. It was based almost entirely on the stories my mother told me. My mother was, we used to say, an old maid. She was very precise and prim and her sisters were very worldly and different from her. But I wrote that story and Lowell, who was my roommate, said, "Why do you write about such nicey-nice people?" To show him I said to myself, "I'm going to write a story about a woman who is so corrupt that she can't recognize innocence when she sees it." And I wrote the first sentence without any idea of what the story would be. "He wanted no more of her drunken palaver." That was "The Fancy Woman," a story about the discovery of evil, really. It's a common theme in fiction.

Broadway: It's a distinctly different story from any of the others.

Taylor: It's how I happened to write it. I didn't think I knew anything about such people. But then I began to remember growing up and friends of mine whose parents were divorced or living a riotous life. And the whole thing came back to me. You can write if you develop your own little world that you write about; you can write about anything within that little frame.

Broadway: Isn't that a difficult thing to do, to live vicariously or see other people's points of view?

Taylor: Oh, it's very difficult. And that's why it's a challenge to do it in fiction and why I'm apt to feel that I will discover more knowledge or more about my own feelings, you see.

For years I wrote about women and finally I wrote one story about old ladies. I just got fascinated by seeing those old ladies who had lived in a secure life but in a world that was going to pieces in a way. After I wrote a story called "Miss Leonora When Last Seen," I never could write another. That really satisfied me. It was as though in all of those stories I had been trying to say something or discover something of myself.

My father used to say, "There are no old gentlemen in the South. The old ladies seem to go on reproducing old ladies without the old gentlemen." (Laughs.) And it was true. They were all around me when I was growing up. But after I had done that for twenty-five years, I decided, well, I'm going to see now about writing stories from men's point of view. Jane Barnes Casey has written a very good article in the *Virginia Quarterly Review* (Vol. 54, 1978) on how I suddenly began writing about men. And my most recent stories have been about men much more.

Broadway: "The Gift of the Prodigal" and "Porte Cochere" in *The Old Forest* are about old men.

Taylor: Yes. Those are both about men. And "The Old Forest" is about women, but it's about a man thinking about women. This so-called novel that I'm writing is all about an old man about 80 who wants to remarry and his middle-aged children won't allow him to. He's got a lot of money, and they don't want him to remarry—a familiar story. It's a comedy on the surface, as a lot of my stories are. I often start out from jokes I've heard.

I have one story called "Heads of Houses." It began when a woman told me about her and her husband going to visit her parents one summer on Lookout Mountain. He was teaching in Greensboro, and they were going to help look after the parents all summer. After they got there, they got on each other's nerves so—the mother and the daughter, especially over the kitchen—that they concocted a story, pretended they got a telegram from the college ordering them to come back early, and they left. They felt so beastly doing this. And as they went down the mountain, they looked up through the sumac and saw the mother and the father and an old bachelor brother had joined hands and were dancing for joy that they'd gone. (Laughs.)

Well, that appealed to me and I wrote it all completely. And it wasn't any good. My wife said she didn't think it came off and I actually threw it away and then rewrote it. Before I got through writing it, the old bachelor brother, who had just been an incidental character in it originally, had become the central serious figure in that he had no life. These other people were going on and behaving foolishly, but they had lives—I mean husbands and wives and children. But this old bachelor brother was in love with a Catholic girl. And they could never marry because she was already married. It was showing, as some of my stories do, that family life is mighty troublesome and hard. But the people that have no family have less satisfaction in life.

Then there's another story—I think of how my stories often begin with something funny. In Memphis there was a girl, the most beautiful girl you ever saw, the queen of the ball. Everybody in town was in love with her. And a boy from out of town—he'd gone to one of these prep schools or colleges—came to town and took her away from everybody else and married her. And everybody was furious because she was so beautiful.

The night she married a terrible snowstorm came up in Memphis and they couldn't get out of town. They were planning to drive to Hot Springs or something. And they had to stay at the Peabody Hotel. And the son of the owner of the Peabody Hotel let the story out that she got locked in the bathroom. (Laughs.) And all the boys in town were just delighted. He had to go up and help her get out of the bathroom. The door was locked, the lock was—well, I changed it around and it was something else. But it was so funny. I meant it as a serious story but it was a funny story.

Broadway: So "Reservations" is basically a true story?

Taylor: It was sort of, just a funny story people told me. I've always felt that if an anecdote or story sticks with me, that somehow it must be important. You wonder: "Why does that joke or story stick with me and I can't remember other stories? It must have some

significance for me." And I think that's what you are trying to find—
those stories that only you could write, that will give you satisfaction
and explain your life to you some. That's what writing is. It's learning
about yourself.

Broadway: Who or what were the early influences early in your
writing career?

Taylor: When I began writing stories, I read Thomas Hardy and
others, and I felt, "I can write something about that." In fact, the first
story I ever wrote and the first influence on me was a woman named
Barnes, Margaret Ayer Barnes. She wrote a book called *Within This
Present* that was a best-seller back in the '30s when I was a boy. And
it came to our house and I read it and I was amazed by it. It was not
a very good novel. It was slick. It was about scenes of life that I knew
growing up in American cities and being from the country, but mainly
hers were in the cities. I could see that was material you could use
and that I would learn from that. And I read other novels by her.

Many years later, in the '50s, I was teaching at the University of
Chicago and was invited out to lunch one day. I got there and the
other guest was Margaret Ayer Barnes. She was an old lady by that
time and she was perfectly delightful. And the marvelous thing was
that she was so amazed that I knew her works. She hadn't met
anybody in years that had read them. So we had a very good time
together. I never saw her again after that.

Broadway: So reading Margaret Barnes is what really got you
started.

Taylor: Well, that's the sort of thing. I began reading Russian
novels—Turgenev more than anyone—and seeing that the setting
and the life they lived was somewhat like the life I'd known. And then
you begin to notice that certain experiences that you've had, you see,
could go into a novel or a story or a poem.

I think that's one reason that I like when I'm teaching in the South
to have people read a lot of Southern fiction. To let them see in
fiction the world that they know. And all of us have learned from
Faulkner. You've read Faulkner and seen the South as he saw it. And
you've seen some of it like that. I don't think that anyone writing can
be without the influence of Faulkner. Almost anybody from the
South. And so, why not? It's great fun, you see what possibilities are

and what can be done with the paraphernalia of your own life. You see how to interpret it and then you begin writing it.

One of the interesting things, too, in reading Trollope is pretending to read with Tolstoy's eyes. Tolstoy loved Trollope, a fact that is not widely known. It's interesting to read certain scenes and think how Tolstoy must have loved this as he read it. And you see certain scenes in Trollope that are as good as Tolstoy. They are wonderful scenes. They are not serious books, novels, but they have some wonderful passages.

Broadway: It's interesting that you're talking about the Southern writers and the Russian writers while contemplating the influences on your own work. What specific things, say, would you see in Faulkner that you see also in Turgenev or Tolstoy or Chekhov?

Taylor: I think it's in the relation of the characters to the context of the story of their lives and other stories and novels. How the characters are is most significant because they lived when and where they did. That to me is the most important thing in serious fiction: the relationship of character to setting, if you will, or to the world or to the context of their lives.

It's very easy to see and demonstrate in Chekhov. In the Chekhov plays and in the stories, too, everything among the gentry, at least, is going to pieces. The farm is not working properly. Or they can't get horses when they want to go to town because the horses are working in the fields. And they're not making any money off the farms. Economically and socially the world is in decline. The characters' lives are unsatisfactory in a way. Masha is in love with Ivan and Ivan is in love with Maria and nothing is working. That's the reason that it is so moving and poetic. The poetry of fiction is the coincidence of the context, the life they're in. Just by instinct the writer picks characters that are significant in terms of the context.

Ibsen's plays—where in that gloomy northern light of Scandinavia there are suicides—in that world, that bleak life they live in and their lives are bleak, there is a coincidence. But when Shaw tries to rewrite Ibsen in one of his plays, it doesn't work. It doesn't have the same meaning when placed in the content of booming Edwardian England that is ruling the world. The people's depression doesn't seem to have the same impact. It's the coincidence that's the poetry of the characters in the world they live in. Oh, in Hemingway, you can really demonstrate it.

Of course if one thing is true in art and literature, the opposite can always prove to be true to some extent. When you say James's characters and Hemingway's characters are often found out of their native context, out of America, the very point is that they're in Europe where everything is different. The morals, the values, are all different.

Broadway: So the setting, the place in Southern fiction is paramount?

Taylor: To me, yes.

Broadway: The culture and setting, then, you find the characters that fit into that setting and interact with it?

Taylor: After the fact it's very easy to look back and say this is what I intended to do. I think what it is, though, is that the writer must be fascinated by the story. As Gertrude Stein might have said, the storyteller is the storyteller is the storyteller. And that must come first. What's happened in this country is that fiction is such a popular form that a lot of intellectuals have said that's the form to write in, to get the ear. And so they write stories and put symbols in and all this. But unless they really love life itself and the characters and love to tell stories, it's not going to work. This is what is marvelous about Faulkner. He knew Mississippi cold.

Broadway: And he didn't give a damn about anybody else, did he? (Both laugh.)

Taylor: He said a lot of foolish things about fiction. But that didn't make any difference because he knew it and got it right. This must be true of any writer. They must first like to tell a story. You know Frank O'Connor said of Joyce—Frank O'Connor didn't like Joyce and was very critical of him—he said that in writing a story, at some point the story must take over. You begin to write it just because it's a story and then it takes over and it means something. And he said, "Whoever heard of a Joyce story taking over?"

He's right. Joyce always has his firm hand on the stories and there's never the feeling of life in it, at least not as much as in O'Connor's. That's what O'Connor is wonderful at—giving a feeling of the lives of the peasants of Ireland and the world they lived in.

And Joyce does it in some stories, but usually you feel that the idea is the main thing. On one hand, that gives his stories a great advantage, because intellectually his stories are much more interesting to people than O'Connor's. But I think he came to a dead end. *Ulysses* and *Finnegans Wake* seem to me a great wasted effort. How many people have ever read *Finnegans Wake* from beginning to end? I know I haven't. In the first place, I'm not a good enough linguist. To really get it, you have to know everything from Gaelic to Greek. It's all right, but it cuts out a lot of readers.

Broadway: It sounds as though you still nurture your mind on classic nineteenth century writers. Do you read many contemporary authors?

Taylor: I'm a great admirer of some of my contemporaries, as far as short story writers are concerned. One is J.F. Powers. I just love him. Talk about little known! He's written only one short novel, and he's written some wonderful stories, one called "The Prince of Darkness." He lives in St. Paul. I have corresponded with him, off and on, for forty years, but I've never met him. And I would love to. He's so witty.

Powers is a Roman Catholic—he was going to be a priest, I think—and most of his stories are about priests and nuns living in the Midwest. It doesn't seem likely, but it's so marvelous, they could only be priests and nuns living in the Midwest. And the young priest is always very liberal and the old monsignor is very reactionary, doing everything wicked. (Laughs.) And the young priest is feeling guilty for having taken a check from some place. And the nuns are exploited terribly by the priests and you see the nuns on Sunday afternoon praying and counting the money for the church. And the old priest is sitting on the front porch, having a can of beer, and the young priest is going out to play golf. The comparison of the lay life is always there, but very strongly it's men and women and their relationships. It's very Aristotelian, finally.

I like Malamud's stories very much. Some of his stories are just excellent—I like them much better than his novels. And I like Hemingway's stories *much* better than his novels; some of them are real poems. I like Faulkner's stories better than his novels; some of his stories, I think, there is nothing in the world better than. Then, I like the novels, too.

Powers is just about my age, and so is Malamud. My friends have mostly been poets, and from the time I was very young my teachers were mostly poets. Ransom and Tate. We became close friends after I graduated from college. But my close friends were Lowell and Jarrell, in school. And we were very close, Lowell and I, for thirty or forty years from the time we were in college till the day he died. And were friends and spent lots of time together. I know a lot of the others and I read a lot of the others.

Broadway: What about Eudora Welty?

Taylor: Oh, I'm crazy about Eudora Welty. We published our first stories in the same issue of the same magazine, a little magazine called *River* published at Oxford, Mississippi. *River* was a little magazine that went for about three issues and I had stories in two. I know Eudora did. That would have been about 1938, maybe 1937. (Taylor published "The Party" in the March 1937 issue and "The Lady is Civilized" in the April issue.) And then we published almost simultaneously in the *Southern Review,* and the old *Southern Review.*

I think Eudora's greatest work is her stories. If you've written novels, that's what everyone knows. The general public knows *Losing Battles, The Ponder Heart,* and *The Optimist's Daughter.* But Eudora's greatest stories are in the two volumes *Curtain of Green* and *The Collected Stories.* I think she is a wonderful story writer. She's one of my absolute favorites.

Broadway: What do you think of Flannery O'Connor's work?

Taylor: I'm an admirer of her stories, too, and I remember her from a very early time. In fact, when she was still a student at Iowa, she sent a story for a contest we had at Greensboro. Later we had her down there and she was marvelous fun to be with. And her remarks. Once somebody asked her on the panel, "What do you think about *Madame Bovary?*" She said, "Haven't read it." (Laughs.) "And I don't need to." That was all she said. She was a very funny person and a very profound one. And her stories were.

Broadway: What do you think Cheever was trying to accomplish? Was he writing in a similar way that you write, about his culture and his community?

Taylor: Perhaps so. It seems more on the surface. I think, though, that he was more concerned with the cultural and social aspects—making a comment on it. To me, the cultural and social aspects of the South are just the tables and chairs and furnishings of life. That's not what my stories are about. They're about what the lives of men and women are like and what they feel and how they respond to each other. The characters certainly are not themselves constantly aware of the social and class structure.

And the blacks and whites—it's inevitable—the blacks and whites are dramatic. I would like to think that in my stories, finally, that the blacks come through much more as people than as blacks. And that was their role in the story and that they suffer from this juxtaposition with whites. But, you see, when I began writing those stories I wasn't thinking, "Oh, I must go out and save the blacks from the whites because the world is destroying them." I didn't feel that at all. I just knew a lot of stories.

Once, after I wrote about blacks for a while, I had to stop because of the '60s—not the '60s, integration. It seems to me that in a war, which integration was like, you can't write about the war because it becomes propaganda. And it's very hard to go on writing just about blacks and whites as though it's just incidental that they're blacks and whites. They're bound in this historical situation and it's all very significant. But it's the furnishings of their house, is what it is. I didn't set out to improve the black man's lot. Or improve woman's lot.

Broadway: One of my favorite stories in your new collection is "Bad Dreams."

Taylor: Yes, that's one of my favorites, too.

Broadway: The struggle is that of a young black couple, but they could just have easily been white in the house, rather than out there above the garage."

Taylor: Yes, that's my feeling about it. That's the way I like to think of that story and that's why I think it's a good story. It remains primarily about those characters and their idiosyncracies and their aspirations. And they behave very badly toward that old black man, but because of what happens they finally just accept it. It is a social comment partly, but it's mainly just that people are caught in these human situations. The story's more about their being human than about their being black.

Broadway: The title "Bad Dreams." There is a certain dreamlike quality to many of your stories that carries the reader to a different dimension of feeling. Why is that? Do you think it's because they are reflections so much of the time?

Taylor: Well, I have this almost Kafkaesque aspect of my work. I like to get that element in it, I must say, because life seems that way to me so much of the time. (Laughs.) I appreciate your observing that, because that's the sort of thing I feel that the man writing in *The New York Times* didn't observe—these atmospheres in the stories and the attitudes about the people. That's what I'm concerned with in that story.

You know that's something real out of my life—that old carriage house or garage, where they live upstairs and the light in the hall, the almost eerie feeling about all that out there. It gave me satisfaction to write it because it reflects feelings that I had with my family in St. Louis. That was the life I lived growing up, and we were always going back to Tennessee. Many weekends and every Christmas, Easter, or summer we'd be down there. My father was a lawyer and businessman and all.

We had this house full of servants. The black house man was named Basil Manley Taylor. One of my forebears was Basil Manley (one of the founders of Furman University in Greenville, South Carolina). And my great-grandfather was Basil Manley Taylor. The Manleys had been Roman Catholics. And Basil Manley left the Catholic Church and became a Baptist and his father never spoke to him again.

Anyway, I don't think I have it in the story. But one time a woman from a family connection, an old lady—Miss Latta Jetton—a very elegant old lady came to visit us in St. Louis. Miss Latta Biggs, she had been as a girl. She was an old lady then, and these servants were much younger and she arrived and her trunk came, an old wardrobe trunk that was sent upstairs.

And Basil, we called him B.M.—we didn't know in those days—he started sending it back and said, "There's no Miss Latta Ton here." He was still thinking of her as Miss Latta Biggs, which had been her maiden name back in Tennessee. She'd been married before he was born, but she was still called Miss Latta Biggs. That's the sort of world we lived in, all very Southern and all very much limited.

When the Depression came my father lost so much. We went back to Memphis. We had a few things, not much money. We were very broke. But you know during the Depression, even in Memphis, you had servants because you only paid them about $2 a week and they were glad to get three meals a day. They lived over the garage, and often when we were very broke we had two servants doing the work.

Broadway: In "The Old Forest" Nat says that despite the things that happened in life after his experience with Lee Ann Deehart, many of them tragic, the impressions of that earlier time remain the most vivid forty years later. Did you have an experience in your youth that had a similar impact?

Taylor: Well, it wasn't all rolled into one, the way Nat's is. I had many experiences, when I was young and going with girls and as Pirandello says, "girls, cigarettes, wine." That's all the paraphernalia of my life at that period. I did have an accident. I got out of the car and fainted. And I was studying Latin. But, you see, I just used those things and the different girls.

Let me give you another example. "In the Miro District" tells the story of a boy hiding a girl in his grandfather's wardrobe. Several years ago I went to a great big antebellum house called Hundred Oaks being sold down at Winchester, Tennessee. I had all sorts of connections with it, and I was going through that day and saw a lot of people I know from Tennessee. I just know so many people because I lived in Nashville and Memphis. And my mother was from Bristol and Johnson City and Chattanooga. And a girl came up to me. She had been a very cute red-headed girl when she was young, and she still looked pretty good. She came up with her husband—I had never met her husband and hadn't seen her in years. And we fell into each other's arms and she said, "I want you to tell Jack that I was not that naked girl."

Broadway: Had you gone out with her and she'd been a girlfriend?

Taylor: Oh, yes, she had been in Nashville. She was a funny, attractive girl.

Broadway: What's happening to the old man in that story? Is he just finally caving in to the expectations?

Taylor: He's defeated. My notion—I don't know—is that he's held onto this one thing, this boy, his grandson, and the grandson feels they're in a different world. The old man could understand a lot about his grandson's life and about the way he can reproach him when he had those wild girls in for the party. But the thing that got him, finally, was that he was sleeping with this girl, a so—called "nice" girl, his girl. That was totally different. It was as though all his standards of behavior had been brought into question.

Then he just didn't care and he was just willing to play the role that they'd set up for him, the old Southern colonel. I saw someone like him. One of the greatest events when I was young was the Confederate reunion. All the Confederates would show up in their uniforms. My grandfather was buried in his uniform, and my Uncle Will was buried in his uniform.

I've never written about this, but Uncle Will studied art and architecture at The University of Virginia and came back to West Tennessee and built a house, a replica of the pavilions on the lawn in Charlottesville. During the war he was shot through the hand at Shiloh and his hand was always paralyzed. As a result he couldn't be an artist and he went west to California and Oregon. He never came back except to visit. But he was there for the Confederate reunion.

He would be at our house, and he had a special wooden fork made that looked like scissors. And it just fit over his fingers, you see, so he could eat with it. I was just a tiny child, and to me that claw of a hand was terrible. He was very difficult and mean and people always excused him, saying, "After the War, he could never be what he wanted to be." Well, it's a typical Civil War story, and it may be true. In due respect, he never could go on with his career.

Those were my earlier days and people don't realize how important such things were to me as a child. We used to go out to the yard and play and pick up little mini-balls and cannonballs in the lawn from the Battle of Franklin that took place near Nashville.

Broadway: On one hand, the old man in "In the Miro District" wants the tradition of moral standards and, yes, he is finally destroyed by the grandson's violation, of never being able to be close to him. Isn't it ironic that he also has been an individual who has been defying, for whatever reasons, the tradition of the old Confederates returning and getting promotions in rank?

Taylor: No. It's the same thing. He wouldn't do any of these things that they wanted him to do. But his family would have loved it if he'd been called "Colonel" instead of whatever he was.

Broadway: In the story "The Old Forest" there are some scenes in bars. And the same is true in "The Other Times," where the uncle and the niece are in the same dive with the boar's head. And he helps the young people escape when the place is raided. It sounds like you must have been there.

Taylor: Oh, yes. That story's all true. I met some of the same kind of people that are in "The Old Forest." In fact, when he made the film, Steve Ross took some of the scenes from that story, "The Other Times," and used them in the film. The old man was a taxidermist and had stuffed dogs. Steve couldn't get any stuffed dogs so he got stuffed pigs. (Laughs.) It was a very good idea to have a place that they go and to see them going out dancing and so on. I went to Memphis and taught last fall for three months at Memphis State, just because it would be fun to see all that again. It was a great experience.

Broadway: Did you go back to any of these places or try to find them?

Taylor: Of course they're all gone now. Steve went out and found places to go. I didn't go to any, but I saw some of the people that had been my friends during that period in life. It was very strange to see them. I hadn't lived in Memphis for forty years. It might have been awful, but it was fun. One thing that's always interesting to me is the differences between Nashville and Memphis. In the old days Nashville always looked down on Memphis as a tough river town. Once I told somebody in Nashville that I had been out to dinner in Memphis twenty-one nights in a row. He said of Memphis—I felt like Henry James —"Twenty-one nights in a row? I didn't know there were twenty-one houses in Memphis for a man to haunt." (Laughs.) Nashville was very starchy in the old days. Country music has changed that image a bit.

Broadway: Your not having lived in Tennessee in so long must make the modernity much more striking when you go back.

Taylor: Yes, it does. Probably much more. But my parents lived there until just a few years ago, and I went back all through the years my brother and sisters were there. It's fun. And Sewanee and Monteagle are such extensions of Nashville. It's the closest high ground, you know, in summer. And so many people I've known come up there. So I don't feel that I've been estranged or really away, entirely.

Broadway: What about the changes that cities like Memphis and Nashville have gone through?.

Taylor: Well, this is what I'm writing about in my novel. When I lived in Memphis, there were 300,000 people. Now there are 900,00. It's just an enormous city. And I describe it as being like an old walled city, within the large but *old* part of town. Nobody's married in or out of that setting in forty years. Somebody might be married a second or third time, but they would be married to somebody in that old part of town.

When I taught at Memphis State, the people there looked upon old Memphis as that walled city. And I remember I was in line at the bursar's office one day and I heard somebody say, "I met somebody last night, said he was from old Memphis and he was from the cotton economy and you know how they are." So you get the new people that have moved in from all over the world. And the old line, the Memphis Country Club, is now right in town. The town goes on for miles beyond. It's no longer a country club. But it has a huge golf course in it. And it was fun seeing how all that is changed.

I have some close friends I see when I go back now. A lot of them are people who teach at Southwestern or Memphis State, and some of them are painters. I have a lot of artist friends. But then I did see some of the old gang and it was great fun. I was a little nervous and thought it might be somehow an unpleasant experience, but it wasn't. It was altogether interesting to me.

Broadway: Do politics hold any interest for you?

Taylor: Not terribly. Most of my friends are much more political than I am. Again, I regard politics almost like the furnishings of a house, that it's part of the world. See, I grew up in a terribly political family. Things were so wretched that finally my mother made a rule that nobody at the dining room table could ever mention politics or religion. My father was very plain spoken.

My sister's husband, who I was crazy about, had a marvelous name, Millsaps Fitzhugh. He was from Mississippi and was very much in the campaign against Crump. And my mother's father had been a senator from Tennessee. So we were in Washington a lot. My mother and father married in Washington. There were always a lot of relatives there. A lot are still there. My grandfather's father was in Washington. My family has always been in politics, but I had a feeling of boredom about it.

As far as being in real politics—as far as being liberal or con-

servative, in the old days, when I was in school—we were not so
much involved as a lot of others of my generation. I had friends who
were very much in the left wing in New York. Going to Kenyon
College partly was an isolating experience. Lowell and Jarrell and I
were all there and seemed far away from the war in Spain and all the
things that were going on.

I was always, I suppose, very liberal in one sense, and very
conservative in another. I've always been very protective of the South
from the liberals. When I met Delmore Schwartz when I was in New
York, just before going overseas, he said, "Why are you Southerners
so mean to Negroes?" I said, "How do you do?" And I hated his
guts. I've found that I've always resented someone's being very
critical of another country or another part of the world that he didn't
know much about. Even when I was in England I was always
resentful of the things Englishmen said about Americans.

I feel about the South as I do about my family. It's all right for me
to criticize and say anything I want to. On the other hand, I think the
pressure on the South is good for it. During the 60's, when integration was going on, I was very resentful of things that were said and
the ignorance that was shown about it. Because at the same time,
blacks were being treated just as badly in New York City.

In fact, one of my friends, a writer, said to me when they were
having so much trouble in New York: "The thing I hate so much
about the South is they treated the blacks so bad. They sent them all
up here and now they are giving us trouble." And he didn't think
anything about it. He was such a Christian.

Broadway: Speaking of subjects you were prohibited from talking
about, what about your religious background? How were you
brought up and what role, if any, does religion play in your life now?

Taylor: When I was growing up we went to the nearest church. My
family was not very religious, and my father was anti-church most of
the time. We had had religious wars, as a matter of fact, on both sides
of the family. Religion was almost outlawed. My father's family had
been Catholics and became Methodists, then Baptists and then
weren't anything. My mother's father was married three times. His
first wife was a Presbyterian, the second a Methodist and the third an
Episcopalian. My grandfather was actually divorced from his third
wife over the issue of religion.

Yet my parents were conventional people, and I went to the Methodist and Presbyterian and Episcopal Sunday schools in St. Louis, Nashville and Memphis. Religion doesn't come up in my stories much. I suppose partly because by the time I came along we had very little drama in our life about it. It didn't play a role with us at all.

Broadway: Some critics in the field of religion and literature contend that a writer does not have to be talking about the church or about God to be a religious writer. Would you consider yourself a religious or spiritual writer without the conventional trappings?

Taylor: I was a religious child, almost in reaction to my parents. I'd never been christened and never had been baptized in the Methodist or Episcopal or any church. But I was always very much interested in religion and the discipline of the church. When I was overseas, I had a chaplain and was baptized and confirmed by the Bishop of Bath and Wells in a little town called Stokes Southampton. But my religion was Aristotelian. It was more of a philosophical idea.

Broadway: At what age were you baptized?

Taylor: It was in 1944 when I was a soldier; I was 27. Lowell and I were very much interested in religion and the church when we were in school. Then, after college, we both went down to Louisiana, and he was converted in Baton Rouge to Catholicism. But he had been reading a lot before then. He had been brought up in the Episcopal Church, strictly.

Broadway: When you talk about values and the past, and there is an interplay there, I never really get the sense that you are a pure—if at all—Agrarian, that you want to go back to those values.

Taylor: They are wonderful values. The thing is, you use them in stories as a way of finding out what people are like. I'm very sympathetic, or I was, to the Agrarians' ideas. But I think it is a *truly* lost cause because of what's happened in the world. It did give us the right relation to God and to nature and to man. But I don't believe it's possible to return to an agrarian civilization under the present circumstances. In 1940 it was much more conceivable than it is now. Those were the ideas that dominated my young manhood, my thought, when I was beginning to write. But even in the stories that touch on them, I had some skepticism.

Broadway: How strong is the theme of disintegration of the family in your stories?

Taylor: It's one of the things that I'm most interested in, and felt most. I think it's terrible, and any society that doesn't have the family as a basic cultural and economic unit is a barbarian dunghill. I think that we don't have it; it's going fast. Even bringing up children—it is very hard to bring up children in a world where the government and society in general don't support the family as a unit. It's not the basic economic unit. It's not as useful the way it once was when you had a small farm and a small business and the family was economically the basis of society. When it becomes something else, it becomes very hard for you to be called upon to play the role of a father in such a society.

For one thing, the consolidation of schools has taken children away from their family and their small community and put them among great *herds* of people just their own age. This is partly what I was touching on with "Miss Lenora When Last Seen." I used to say to my students during the '60's: "It's very easy to love everybody who is just your own age. That kind of commune is very easy. You go and sympathize with others. But to be in a commune with a family, in which you have people of all ages, that's much more complicated and much deeper."

I remember feeling in the '60s that parents had no support from church or school. And any authority you had over your children you had—not through tradition, as the father and head of the family and part of society organized that way—you had authority by force of will, assertion. That is a very ugly role. And it's different from the authority of the father as established by tradition, that you respect him. You don't have it unless society and tradition support it. Otherwise, in every case, as soon as the child is able to tie his shoes, he will be more a part of the peer group, as they call it. This is part of what I'm writing about in some new stories.

Broadway: How do we cope with this constantly changing modern society where values seem to be in such decline?

Taylor: It's a desperate situation. Economically, the family is not feasible anymore. And so we turn to things like Marxism. Children are taken off and raised by the state and the quality of life that arises from individual relationships is lost. It's unknown. We're going into something that's never existed before, except maybe in primitive societies where families were not as strong and the children were raised by the tribe.

It was much healthier in the extended family in the old order where you had grandmothers and aunts around than when the child focuses entirely on his parents as his only authority. When I was a child, you could turn to other aunts and uncles and old colored people. It wasn't just all mother and father. It was the whole family. But in the modern family you have one child and a couple and there is nobody else. It's all between them.

Broadway: You say you're working on some new stories about these issues. Does that mean you're writing beyond the '30s and '40s, when most of your stories are set?

Taylor: Everything that I write now focuses more on the present— since the Second War, at least—but it goes back and forth. What I like to do is to play back and forth between the past and the present as much as possible. I would like to write stories about generational differences, about the present generation. A lot about the present generation. I've taught young people for so long. I say that maturity is forgiving parents. I had great grievances against my father, but I didn't in the end before he died.

Broadway: What changed that?

Taylor: Just seeing what it was like to be a grown man and having children of my own, and him no longer controlling me. When I wanted to go to college, he wanted me to go to Vanderbilt, and I didn't want to go to Vanderbilt. I wanted to go to Columbia University where I had a scholarship. And we had a knockdown, dragout quarrel and stopped speaking. The trunk was packed and I was going. My mother supported me—you know how mothers always support you. But he wouldn't give in, and I didn't give in.

I got a job on the newspaper in Memphis and didn't go to college. But then I went to Southwestern, where Tate was teaching, and took some courses while I was working. And Tate persuaded me to go to Vanderbilt, because he'd gone there and studied with Ransom. I went off to Vanderbilt. Then Ransom left Vanderbilt and went to Kenyon. And I followed him and my father agreed to that. He had known Ransom.

Broadway: Wasn't it a year before you went to Kenyon?

Taylor: That's right. I went home and Ransom went up there. Half the year I took courses at Southwestern—philosophy and history courses, mostly. And then Mr. Ransom got me a scholarship.

Broadway: What other works do you have in progress?

Taylor: Mainly I have been working on the novel. But in parts. It may not be a novel. I don't know whether I can write a novel. But it's going to be as big as a novel.

And then I'm working on plays. I've always wanted to write plays. And I've written a collection of short plays. I published in book form one play. My plays have only been done in little theaters and on local television. *A Stand in the Mountains* is about to come out as a book in a revised form. Frederic Beil, the man who brought out a new edition of *A Woman of Means,* is going to print it.

He lives in New York, but he's from Sewanee. That's how he knew about my work. And that's why he published William Alexander Percy. I knew Mr. Will Percy. He had a summer house at Sewanee and so did Walker Percy growing up. It was his uncle, Mr. Will, who brought him up.

In fact, the three plays I've been working on—I have one that's finished—all have the same setting, which is Sewanee and Monteagle. That's become a wonderful vehicle for me, because it's where all the South gathered in the summertime, and when everything else had changed, it was very much the same up there.

One of the plays is a reworking of *A Stand in the Mountains.* A "stand in the mountains" is what some people wanted Robert E. Lee to do at the end of the war, to go into the mountains and take a stand. And he could've held out, they said, for years. And that's what this is called. This is the South's last stand. The title comes from Donald Davidson, who has a poem about Robert E. Lee and their wanting him to make a stand in the mountains.

Another of the three I'm working on is a literary play. I have literary characters because for years, during the war, just before and after, a lot of literary people stayed at Monteagle. It was a very cheap place to stay during the winter, you see, and Allen Tate and his wife had a house there for two years. Robert Lowell and Jean Stafford came down. Andrew Lytle was there. In fact, it was there that my wife and I met and married. We were visiting the Tates there and we were married at Sewanee. It's a place I'm very much interested in, and I find it endlessly interesting.

Broadway: What's the third play?

Taylor: It's about another family. It was in one of those cottages in the summer and it's sort of a continuation of the novel I've written. My father—I'll tell you a little story that was the basis of it—my father was in business in Nashville and St. Louis and we had a house in Nashville, a horse farm we'd go back to. My father was a lawyer, and his principal client and a friend of his from college was Rogers Caldwell, who was the biggest financier in the South. He had a huge empire, but it turned out they were doing some very crooked things. And my father felt such an idiot because he was their lawyer, right in the middle of it all.

Later he realized that they had gotten him to go to St. Louis so that he couldn't see what was going on in Nashville. And then the whole thing blew up in the crash of 1929. They'd been gambling with other people's money, was what it was. And my father was a great fox hunter and sportsman, horseman. He and Caldwell had been the closest friends for many years and Caldwell completely deceived him. After that my father said he would never live in the same town as Rogers Caldwell, and we didn't mention his name.

Years later, on my porch at Monteagle one summer we were there—my parents were over at the hotel—and Rogers Caldwell and my father met again after twenty-five years of not speaking. And they just fell on each other. From that day on they were on the telephone almost daily. So that's what my third play is about. I haven't worked it all out. I change my ideas about it.

Broadway: It's a wonderful story.

Taylor: Well, it was a marvelous story to me. I was so involved in all that, growing up. It had a *big* effect on my life, and so all of the details came back. Things that are important came back. When the money was gone we moved back to Memphis, and then my father made another big go of it. He owned a lot of land and became happy again after that. I guess he was forty-five when we moved back to Memphis. He's the one that I make into the old man who wants to remarry. You write, and then you combine these things and get a dramatic effect. It's a way of just idling your time, partly playing with little details and things that fascinate in life. A lot of it's just silly, but it's great fun.

Broadway: A critic writing about your collection of plays called *Presences* commented that their "ghost story" aspect was more psychological than supernatural and noted the influence of the Japanese *Noh* plays.

Taylor: I'm not sure they come under the umbrella of *Noh* plays. Perhaps, but not consciously, anyway. They are ghost stories. But they're all psychological stories.

Broadway: Jamesian?

Taylor: Jamesian. That's the big influence. And there's one that's just a steal. You know you want something so much you often don't realize it. I have one phrase that I know I lifted from Katherine Anne Porter and I can't remember where it is. But I didn't realize I was doing it. But then later I knew that I'd gotten that out of one of her stories. There's one play—I didn't set out to do it, but I don't deny it, James's story called "The Jolly Corner"—and it's about a man coming back to St. Louis and meeting himself. Dealing with ghosts in a play is a fun vehicle. In fiction you've got to prepare for the ghost for pages and make it right, whereas in a play you just say, "Enter ghost." Of course, a lot of things are harder. It's got to be dramatically right. And the lines have got to be sufficiently, intrinsically interesting.

Broadway: How did you get interested in the supernatural?

Taylor: I've always had a curiosity about ghost stories. I came to realize from reading and from my own experience that people who see ghosts see them because they need to see them, or want to see them. The wish is so strong or the need is so strong. I remember people when I was a child who saw ghosts and told me about them. And of course this is what James did not only in "The Jolly Corner," but also in the famous short novel *The Turn of the Screw.* And so I began to cast about and to think about these things in one little scene that would take chapters in a piece of fiction. It's just too apparent that the great short story writers have also been playwrights instead of novelists. Chekhov wrote great plays and Pirandello wrote stories and great plays. And the Irish playwrights were also short story writers.

Broadway: And you think that's more than chance?

Taylor: I think that's more than chance. I think there's a real affinity there. Short story writers are *pressed* by publishers to write novels. And there's not theater in this country. They have nowhere to turn in writing plays because we don't have theater. I mean on the level of our literature or our painting. Our literature particularly, our poetry and fiction, is as sophisticated and good as there is.

Broadway: Who is going to publish your novel?

Taylor: Well, I have a contract with Knopf.

Broadway: You have quite a reputation for taking months and even years to write your stories. Has Knopf given you any sort of deadline for the novel?

Taylor: Oh, heavens. I've had this contract for several years. I have the book finished. It's just a matter of reworking some parts. It's not a good idea for me to ever push a story. I keep them around for years just tinkering with them. And then get a second inspiration. And forget them and come back to them. I like to do that. In all the years I've been writing I've done that.

Broadway: Would you consider being published by a publishing firm in the South?

Taylor: My wife has a new book of poems, *Selected Poems,* which has been brought out by Stuart Wright in Winston-Salem. And he's just beginning. And of course Chapel Hill is beginning to do some things. It's a great time for little publishers to take over. Big-time New York publishers are having a hard time economically and many have been bought out by Gulf Oil or other conglomerates. Very few of them are owned by themselves or make their own judgments. Poetry is having a *much harder* time. Even people like Robert Penn Warren.

The squeeze is on at the publishing houses to make every book a seller, to make money. The last time I was in New York, I was in the dining room of the Gramercy Park Hotel. Three men who'd been jogging, youngish men, came in and were talking. I was seated alone at the next table and eavesdropped on their whole conversation. One was a man from something like Gulf Oil and the other men were publishers and he was laying down the law for them.

He said, "You are a fashion house and you're going to print what is fashionable and what people want. We've got to get a different distribution system and different editor." They were making excuses and he was just blasting them. It was almost like something made up.

If it happens in one publishing house, it happens in another. It's a great opportunity for little publishing houses to get hold of young poets and fiction writers. This is partly what Stuart Wright is doing and what Frederic Beil is doing.

Broadway: Your stories are so heavily centered around people and events of thirty or forty years ago. Do your experiences now, say in Gainesville and Charlottesville, build on that core?

Taylor: Well, to some extent. I have another completely practical life, in which I am interested in real estate, and all my friends in Charlottesville will have nothing to do with any of this, you see. We went to a party here the other night where we were taken as a matter of fact. It was a big reception held for the preservation of old districts; somebody knew what our history was and took us to it. And we just had a grand time talking to the people there. Many Southern types.

Eleanor at one time looked over at the bench and said to me, "See those three old ladies there? I want to meet them. I just know their life history by looking at them." And she did. After awhile they came one by one and we got in a circle together and talked. They were just exactly what we had speculated. And one of them knew intimately a woman in Charlottesville that we knew. Of course, most of my literary friends don't have this interest in the past. In a way it's a hobby and an escape. (Laughs.) Hemingway had his hunting, and I have the world of the bourgeois, the old gentry.

Broadway: How are you enjoying Gainesville?

Taylor: It's been so cold this winter. I mean for us. I'm a strange case. I have arthritis terribly and after a certain threshold. . . . Well, in Charlottesville the last two years I was going around on crutches. There's something they call dry arthritis, and when it hits I become this ancient, crippled creature. It's as though I become Dr. Jekyll and Mr. Hyde.

So that's why we bought this house. We think it's nice in the winter, in the coldest months, to go off and hibernate and write. I like Charlottesville a lot, but it's nice to get away from it.

And I like Gainesville. I have a number of friends here. Alistair Duckworth in the English department at the University of Florida—he used to be at Virginia; Robert Ray, a young poet; and a younger writer whose work I like very much, Padgett Powell, who published a book this year called *Edisto* about the island right off Charleston. We have some great friends here, the Kirby-Smiths, who really are from Sewanee.

And my wife's sister's husband is the poet Don Justice. We've been close since we all married about forty years ago. We got him to Charlottesville for a year just a few years ago, so I came down to visit and we thought we'd try North Florida. It's been pretty successful.

Broadway: But you'll return to Charlottesville for the summer?

Taylor: Yeah, that's our home. I can't quite give up Charlottesville. I've taught there nearly twenty years, you see. When I went out there, I thought Charlottesville was sort of a snooty place and I wouldn't like it long. But I liked my students and I love the country around Charlottesville. I think even more I like the Valley of Virginia over at Lexington and Warm Springs.

Broadway: Would you talk more about your real estate ventures?

Taylor: We fancy old houses and have restored at least eight or ten from around the 18th century. It's a great joke among my friends. They call it my "real estate dealings." They know better, but that's their way of teasing me and because none of them are really interested in it very much.

We began very early, when we were first married. My wife is from a little place called Norwood, North Carolina, in the country. The first house we moved into we restored was her family house, a wonderful 18th century house. Then we bought a house in Hillsboro, the Colonial governor's summer town, and lived there a number of years. And so we've gone on and on.

We've done four or five 18th century houses in the neighborhood of Charlottesville. We once moved into a pretty stone house out from town with a big kitchen and yard. Then I had a heart attack. By the time I got out of the hospital my wife had moved us back into Charlottesville.

Broadway: Do you live in the houses you restore?

Taylor: Well, this is what my friends kid us about because most of these houses are old shackledy places. You can't call them houses. Usually we don't live in them; it's just a hobby. We keep one going, then get tired of it and sell it for some reason or another.

I call mine out from Charlottesville "The Ruins." It's a brick house built around 1780, a little one story and a half house. You know, a little early Virginia brick house with two brick end chimneys. And it has a little English basement with a kitchen down in the basement. The windows are out, so it's not habitable in its present form. I'd been looking and I wanted a ruin, an old brick house on a farm that I could play with. It was just fun looking, searching every old thing that came up for sale. And finally this was just it.

Oh, the land! It's just beautiful out in the field. I had the masons out to rebuild the chimneys. And I built a front stoop and a back stoop—the old kind they used to have.

And we found the old 18th century stone spring house and a little creek that was half dried up. The spring had been sealed up for years, and we got some people out to work on it. They dug down and suddenly they hit. The water that had been backed up shot about twenty feet in the air. We got a big, booming spring that produced about nine gallons a minute.

I like to do landscaping. On the last place I had I built three ponds, one spilling into the other—18th century style. And that's what I've done to this place. It's got great boulders on the side of the hill, rocks as big as this room. And it's very beautiful. I was even building an imitation graveyard, a topiary graveyard with carvings and shrubbery. It was pure folly. And Eleanor's planted acres of trees. Then there are a lot of blackberries, persimmons to be gathered and that sort of thing.

Unfortunately, I've gotten to the point with this arthritis I just can't do as much work. I like to do hard work—I mean dig ditches and put up fences. That's just my weakness. I hate to sell it, but if I can't work on it, I hate to hire people to go out and do all the work.

We've never made any money off our houses, but we've never lost any. So I feel very honorable about it. We just had fun.

Broadway: Do you ever do any of the structural improvements yourselves?

Taylor: We used to. I'm crazy about it. I have young friends who in fact used to be my students. People say that the ones who I gave the best grades to were the ones who liked to restore old houses.

One time I had a cabin down in the Blue Ridge, on the parkway. A writing student and I rebuilt the cabin. It was a chestnut log cabin and we rented the steel scaffolding and took it there. It was silly but fun.

Broadway: This house may be old, but it is far from rundown. Why did you decide to buy it?

Taylor: Gainesville is surrounded by some little towns—shabby looking, decadent Southern towns with a lot of moss and beautiful trees. We went and looked at those places and then looked in this old section from the '20s and earlier. We finally found this house ourselves, and our real estate agent couldn't believe we were going to buy this one after all we had described to her. We suddenly said we had gotten to a certain age and know comfort when we see it.

Broadway: And this house has been remodeled?

Taylor: Yes, I think it was a cinderblock house originally with clapboard siding. Someone had just done it over with a Spanish roof and plaster's been put on around the outside. This living room was a little room they expanded to make a larger room. It has a kitchen and three little bedrooms and two baths.

When we first saw it my wife said, "Oh, that would be so easy to keep." And it has a big yard. My wife is a terrific gardener. And this has such a nice big lot with some big, beautiful live oak trees. In Key West we didn't have live oaks. We just had palm trees and tropical plants. . . .

If you're a gardener, anyplace is interesting because there are entirely different kinds of growth. There's one huge tree out here—do you see that limb with those dried ferns on it? Two days ago they were green and rich. Every time it rains they come out, and then as soon it gets dry, they dry up like that. The first time that happened we thought they were dead, but they came back.

Broadway: Do you do mainly flower gardening or vegetable gardening?

Taylor: A little of both. Flower gardening mostly. There's a huge fern garden around the side of the house. And that's one of the things that attracted us here. See, there's a little creek down there. But this has been the coldest winter on record here, I think, and right now it looks pretty bleak. All these leaves aren't supposed to fall, at least not all at once like this.

Broadway: Did the furnishings come from your house in Charlottesville?

Taylor: We're crazy about furniture. A lot of the stuff—well, some

of it—is my family's. That bench over there was in the house when I
was growing up. I got it when we were married. My family always
called it the Mexican bench because somebody brought it back from
Mexico. And my wife collects old kitchen safes like these.

Some of this furniture had been at Sewanee, in Monteagle, where
my family had a summer place for a long time. My family has been
going to Monteagle for hundreds of years, it seems, and people I've
known for hundreds of years. We have all kinds of relatives in
Monteagle, so it was nice for our children since we lived all over this
country and in Europe to come back there in the summers. That's
where our children knew people—they called them cousins.

Broadway: Do you still have the house in Monteagle?

Taylor: No, we don't. We sold it a few years ago because it was
just—well, you know how these places can get. There's something
somebody's broken, the water pipes burst or something. Finally, you
get a headache from them. And one night you say, "Let's get rid of
it." But we still go back to Sewanee every chance we get. It's very
easy to rent a house there in the summer because it's all faculty, you
know, and they leave.

Broadway: What do you think you'll do now that you can't work
and tinker around as much?

Taylor: I don't know what I can do. I just can't work as much
outdoors. I used to work outdoors from morning to night and loved
it. We have notions of getting away. I've never been to Greece. I've
never been to southern Spain. I've never been to Venice. I've lived in
Italy twice and never been to Venice. And when we used to go to
Europe every year, when I was at Ohio State, the children were
small. When we went to Naples and to Pompeii, I was pushing my
little boy along the cobblestones and he was crying because it was
rough. And I couldn't see the dirty pictures (laughs) because we had
the two children.

We had a good time, but what we did usually was to rent a house.
And we had great luck. Just go and stay for six months. We lived on
the Riviera twice with the Robert Fitzgeralds. They were great friends
of ours and they had children. And the Jarrells went over with us
once. And Jack Thompson did. We rented an apartment in Rome
one winter. We lived it up in those years. We've been back to
London a couple of times, but we haven't done the big things since

we got the children up and out. So, if I can sell some of this real estate. . . .

Broadway: When did you retire from full-time teaching?

Taylor: About two years ago. But I still take short teaching assignments. I did one in Memphis and I'm doing one in Athens this spring. It's fun. My advice to young people is don't teach unless you're gregarious and like people and like to talk. Most of my friends now are former students.

Broadway: Does your teaching help your writing?

Taylor: I think so. It makes me understand it. It doesn't do it immediately, but I think in the long run I have a much better view of what I think fiction is and what I want to put into fiction. And the writers I admire, I begin to understand. Before I taught I didn't know why I liked them in particular.

I love Frank O'Connor. And I like D. H. Lawrence's stories very much and I like Chekhov's stories and Turgenev's stories. While teaching them, you know if you have to get up before a class of people and say why these stories are good stories, you have to come to grips with them. If you read them just for yourself, you might amble off and think about it a lot. But if you don't write it down or teach it, you might never come to a moment when you have to put it into words and say, "It's this for me."

Broadway: How do you teach your creative writing classes?

Taylor: I like to have an undergraduate course in which I read stories that I like and have them read lots of stories. I read Faulkner stories and the usual Hemingway stories and talk about how to put a story together. Undergraduates can be helped a lot by showing them just how to read a story. And then I'll have a graduate class where the students just turn in their own stories. Graduates ought to know how to read.

It's funny, you get students every now and then that would talk so wonderfully that you'd just want to shut up and let them talk because they're so terribly articulate. Then you read their stories and they're not very good. That's what I used to say of people at Harvard. To get into Harvard you've got to have such a high IQ anyway. They all thought they were so smart and they weren't used to me. And if you told them a story was bad, they couldn't believe it.

Being a good writer doesn't mean that you're intelligent or educated. It doesn't mean anything. It's the coincidences of things in your life and your temperament that make the difference.

Broadway: Do you think that students have changed over the years?

Taylor: It's hard to say because I'm not teaching all the time. But I remember the '50s crowd was just as dull as dishwater when I taught during that time at Indiana University and the University of Chicago. Well, Chicago was better.

And the '60s were bad. I got so disgusted during the '60s. All the filth and four-letter words and all that were useless in stories, and sex and so on. And I would curse them and call them heathens, but they were more fun.

And it was just a year before I stopped I did begin to see some of it. A girl in my class came up and complained about a story that had been read in a creative writing class—the language in it—and I couldn't believe it. People are such sheep, you know. Two years before it couldn't have happened. That girl actually complained. No, we didn't read it in class. I xeroxed it on purpose. It was indelicate, but you got so you'd get hardened to it. And often the best thing to do with a story is to xerox it and let the class deal with it. They often come down on it and you don't have to say a word.

Broadway: You said you taught once at the University of Chicago. How long were you there?

Taylor: Only for a quarter. I taught in the English department and I'd write. My wife was crazy about Chicago. We lived near the university in a place called the Midway Plaisance in an old apartment hotel. Our daughter was a tiny thing. I taught and had good students and found it pretty interesting. But it was so cold for me even then. I remember—I taught the spring quarter—it snowed the second day of June. A light snow but still it was that cold. And you know eventually I went and taught at Harvard. I had a permanent appointment at Harvard, and I left Harvard because I just got so cold in the winters.

Broadway: How long did you teach at Harvard?

Taylor: Three years. First I went there as a visiting professor, then came back as a regular. Both of us loved Cambridge, but I was in bed for days. So I just got up one day and went over and resigned. The chairman of the department was offended. He didn't believe any-body could ever resign from Harvard. And really it is the best academic community, I think. He said, "You mean you're resigning?" because I had tenure and he couldn't fire me. He said, "Well, we're not going to hold you as a prisoner." That was his last word to me. And I missed it. I knew I would. I simply couldn't be there.

Broadway: Where did you go after that?

Taylor: I went back to Virginia. Oh, finally I had an appointment. I had a half-year appointment in Virginia and a half-year at Harvard. Harvard in the fall. Then the chairman at Virginia suggested I be at Virginia in the fall. Just being ornery. So I did it. I didn't want to, but I did it anyway. I spent January, February, March in Boston. And the snow got so deep and stayed dirty.

I'll tell you another reason I left Harvard. I thought I was a great success as a teacher. Even Lowell, who was teaching at Harvard, had nothing to do with getting my appointment. He couldn't believe it when I told him I was coming there. I thought I was a great success as a teacher and being at Harvard. But I was known as a fiction writing teacher, and I hated being labeled as a teacher.

Broadway: Labeled as a specific kind of teacher?

Taylor: No, instead of being a writer. See, my teaching of writing was more than my writing to people and I just hated that. I thought I was a failure. There are a lot of famous writing teachers at Harvard who publish a book or so and they're marvelous with students. They go along and that's their life. But that's not being a writer. That's being known as a famous writing teacher who also writes. And I said that I just didn't want to stay on and be at Harvard. And teaching that much. A half-year at Harvard and a half-year at Virginia just occupied me. I didn't do much writing. So I left and came back to Virginia. From then on I just taught a half-year.

Broadway: Hadn't you taught in Greensboro off and on for twenty years?

Taylor: I was there three times. I went to Greensboro right after I got out of the army. I went to New York and worked for a publishing house for a while. Then I decided I'd come down and teach at Greensboro. Eleanor had been to school there, and her old professors got me there. And then Allen Tate had just gone to Greensboro. He was a good friend of mine. We quarreled some once or twice, but we were good friends. I went there in 1946 or '47 right after the war and taught for two years. And I got Jarrell back to

Greensboro. He had been editing *The Nation* and was teaching at Sarah Lawrence.

Then I was invited to go to Indiana University. I went there for one year and hated it. It was so foolish. After the war I was hard to please somehow. And I hated Indiana University. I lived in three different houses and moved around. We had a lot of furniture that we brought up there, so one day I decided "we're not coming back here" and called an auction house to get all our furniture. And we left town without saying anything. If somebody had done that to me later, some young whippersnapper, I would've said that's not ethical. But I did. And you know we didn't put a price on it. We just said auction it off and you know they got $25 for all our furniture. (Laughs.)

We returned to North Carolina where I had a farm and stayed awhile. And I went back to Greensboro again for a couple of years. Then Chicago invited me to teach, and while I was there Kenyon asked and I went and taught at Kenyon. I taught at Kenyon for five years. I had a wonderful time there. I loved it. I had good students, good skiing spots at Kenyon—I could still go outdoors. We got cold and things changed there, the president died or something.

Then I went to Ohio State for six years. And I hated it, in a way. But I was paid a year-round salary: a twelve-month salary and had to teach only from October 1st to February 1st. Absolutely wonderful! But I had terrible students. Because we didn't like Columbus, we went to Europe every year in February.

But my conscience began to bother me. I realized that the only reason I was staying at Ohio State was for the money. I was getting a marvelous salary, but I didn't like it. And I thought, "I'm just here to make money and that's not a way to teach." And students were not very good. In other words, I was using them. So I got in touch with Jarrell. He was still in Greensboro and he got me back there for the third time. I was there for about two or three years. Jarrell killed himself after the third year, I think. It was the very same year he cracked up.

Broadway: His death must have been extra hard on you.

Taylor: It was *very* hard. When I made my first trip to Harvard, I visited Jarrell there, and he was cracking up then. He later called and talked long distance for an hour. He never did that sort of thing. He was talking to me mostly about a review that Jack Thompson had done in *The New York Review of Books*—big, full-page review. And he called me and said, "That's just a terrible review and I'll never speak to him again." It was a relatively good review, but Thompson wrote that I was really a Midwesterner. He read into my stories that these people and the cities in the South were Midwestern. Well, that infuriated Randall, who was not a dyed-in-the-wool Confederate Agrarian by any means, but he took offense.

Broadway: Tell me more about Jarrell.

Taylor: He was a brilliant, brilliant man. I wish I could tell you more. What Lowell and I used to say is that we ought to write down the *witty* things. He said the wittiest things. He was like Shaw about literature. He read so widely and he was so crazy about literature. It was just like life. And teaching. He loved teaching, and he loved teaching women at Greensboro.

He was a marvelous reader of your works. He would go over your stories with wonder, and if he didn't like a story he was offended by you as though you smelled bad. He just couldn't stand it. One summer we were in a little village. I passed Randall downtown and I spoke to him, but he turned away and wouldn't speak to me. And, you know, he was my lifelong friend. I went to Mary, his wife, and said, "What in the hell is wrong with Randall?" And she said, "He doesn't like that new story." (Laughs.) And he didn't. And then years later he would come to me and tell me he did. He had changed his mind, and he liked it.

People would say, "How could you put up with that?" But it was as though you were his friend and this alter ego, this other side of you, had done this terrible thing to this friend of his. He was a wonderful writer. And he was not going to speak to that person that'd done it. And he'd do the same with Lowell. His good friends. He'd just be furious about it, so he couldn't talk about it. He was so angry.

He was devoted and loyal as a friend. It was just wonderful to talk with him about any piece of literature. You could sit here the whole evening and talk about a four-line stanza and he loved it. He wrote the preface to my wife's first book; he would go over her poems, too. For years we were very close, and when he died it nearly killed me.

Broadway: What do you think he was broken by?

Taylor: You can't say what the real reasons are, you know. Like all of us he wanted to be God. He wanted to be the best writer or poet of his time, but he wasn't recognized as such. I mean he was recognized *enormously,* more than I ever have been, but he wasn't satisfied. And there were other things. It was a long, complicated story.

He was a marvelous friend. It made life better. And we were so different. Randall was so intellectual and persistently, exhaustingly literary, just talking all night. Lowell and I had this enormous fun. And Lowell wasn't intellectual in the way that Jarrell was.

It was a great loss—both of them—to me. You feel guilty sort of going on. And also I have a certain anger at them for dying, though not literally.

Broadway: You feel guilty because you think you could have helped them in some way?

Taylor: No, no. Just guilty to be alive and they're not. Yeah. They were enormously talented people. And, you see, we'd all been friends since we were in college and really were very young. I used to visit Lowell and his parents in Boston. He was something of a mother's boy. His mother was a New England type, a Winslow who looked down on the Lowells, who were the newcomers.

And she was a great friend—sort of a pink lady at the institute—of Merrill Moore. Merrill Moore was one of the Agrarians of Nashville who wrote with the Fugitive group. A poet. Brilliant man. Became a psychiatrist. Went to Boston and was Mrs. Lowell's psychiatrist or else she worked with him as an assistant somehow. He saw Cal Lowell really crack up early. And he sent Lowell down to Vanderbilt to stay with Ransom because Merrill Moore had been an early student of Ransom. Moore was a great friend of Robert Penn Warren.

Broadway: What do you think of Ian Hamilton's biography of Lowell?

Taylor: Ian Hamilton is a very good biographer. It's a very solid work, and it's very good. The only reservation I have is that it doesn't get Lowell's sense of humor. He's an English writer, and you know English and American are not the same. One of the things that keeps Lowell from seeming a beast is the sense of humor in his life was so wonderful. He seems a grotesque author. You just read about what he's like, how serious.

He and I stood together on certain issues. In the very beginning, we were conscientious objectors. Our interest in religion was quite genuine over a period of time, and we were able to talk about it. We were always very close. But it was partly the humor, and that's what's sad. Hamilton's book doesn't have it.

I know Ian Hamilton, and he came and stayed with me in Charlottesville while he was writing the book—I mean to talk about Lowell. And Lowell liked and respected him.

Broadway: You said Jarrell wanted more recognition than he had, yet it's a well-known fact that you have not actively sought fame for yourself. How does being famous affect a writer?

Taylor: You know, after people get to be famous it must just be *terrible* meeting people and going on. I remember meeting James T. Farrell when I was about 22 or 23, out at the University of Missouri. Well, I was probably older than that; I'd just published a book. It was at a bookstore and Farrell was so ugly to everybody and insisted on getting in the back room. He was such an egoist, so *rude* to other human beings. But I guess if you're as famous as he was at that time . . .

Broadway: You think it's just a way of coping with success?

Taylor: Yes. He got so sick of people—you know, pushing and pulling and wanting. He shouldn't, of course. It never affects some people that way. Some writers become actors and are above all that. But Farrell was terrible.

Lowell was very difficult to a lot of people, but he didn't *mean* to be. He just couldn't cope with the fame. When he'd come to Virginia, he'd talk to me as though we were still sophomores at Kenyon and say awful things to me—crude, like two little boys who were good friends. It was just water on a duck's back to me, but it offended a lot of my friends that he treated me so badly. And then he also was jealous of my friends; he was rude to all of them.

When I visited him in Boston, he made everybody have me to dinner—the grande dames, all his friends. It was just marvelous. I got to see really inside Boston. But when he came to visit me in Memphis or Charlottesville, he would resent my friends. He was jealous of them; they weren't anybody as far as he was concerned. He was like my father, who my wife always said couldn't accept a present. Lowell didn't know how to respond, didn't want to be on the receiving end. He was a great egoist. But he was very generous as far as I was concerned, so I didn't care about it.

Broadway: Isn't the story "1939" about you and Lowell?

Taylor: It's almost literally true.

Broadway: Who are the two girls?

Taylor: Jean Stafford was his girl and mine was a girl from St. Louis. Jarrell used to say I ought to have just put in the real names, it was so close to life, and make it a memoir. But of course it wasn't; there were things I made more dramatic.

Broadway: What about the fight on the train?

Taylor: That was true. That was literal. We got into a terrible fight. (Laughs.) In our room once he broke my gooseneck lamp because I wouldn't go to bed when he wanted to. We had a big room, and he came over and took my goose-neck lamp and broke it into pieces. (Laughs.) And I wouldn't speak to him. We stayed up half the night just *growling* about it. I was furious after that.

Broadway: Did you ever hurt each other?

Taylor: Not really. On the train that night was the nearest we ever came to it, though. But we were just children. And then we came back to Kenyon and there were all those people in our room, cooking. One of them was in New York the last time I saw him. But it was a very healthy sort of atmosphere. I mean it was when we were boys, still fighting and going on.

There were a lot of advantages to our being near Ransom. And then Tate would come to town, and other writers were coming in there. Ransom, you see, was the teacher of all those people. The Tates, Warrens, Lytles and Davidsons. And he was regarded as the master of all. And he was. He was the center.

Broadway: What made Ransom the master?

Taylor: Well, he had great ability. Of course he was a classicist and a Rhodes scholar and all that. But also there was a great reserve about him he never gave away. He never became too intimate with people. He and I became *good* friends after college. But he had a formal manner of the old school. When I went back to teach at Kenyon, he and his wife and my wife and I played bridge every Friday night. We kept the scores on the closet door of an old house we lived in—men against women. And that went on all the years. When we were in public he insisted on my calling him John. I was on the faculty at the time, so I did. But in private when we were having an intimate conversation it was "Mr. Ransom."

Broadway: For which teacher do you have the most respect?

Taylor: The person who taught me the most was Allen Tate, making me feel that literature was important. And I don't know how he did it. Ransom was wonderful at teaching you to throw no punches and to be tough about making judgments—and with a cold eye. And he had rules. What was so instructive was that he had absolute rules about writing. When you turned in a poem to him the first thing that he did was to go through *abbc, abbc*. He went through the whole thing to make sure the rhyme scheme was true. And then the dum dum, dum dum, and all the elements in the poem. There was great instruction because Ransom talked only about the best literature and you were put up against that.

Tate was much more enthusiastic. The drama of being a writer of literature—that was wonderful for a young man, to make you feel that what you're doing is important. Especially when he liked your work. He liked my work from the beginning. It was just wonderful. It couldn't have been better.

Broadway: I envy you those years and those friendships. It's very unusual to have them both.

Taylor: I was lucky to come along just when I did.

A Composite Conversation with Peter Taylor

Hubert H. McAlexander/March 1985–July 1986

This previously unpublished interview is drawn from conversations with Peter Taylor that began shortly after he
arrived at the University of Georgia as Eidson Visiting
Professor of Creative Writing for the spring quarter 1985.
The setting for Part One is my Southern Literature class,
which Taylor visited twice. Part Two is a composite of
conversations that took place primarily during our fre-
quent lunches. As often as three times a week, we set out
either for some typical college town restaurant, or more
to Taylor's liking an indigenous place like Walter's Pit
Cook Bar-B-Q or the Chase Street Cafe, where an
oldtime, heavy southern midday meal was served in a
small building that reminded him of Key West. Sporting
his favorite straw cap and using one of a number of
interesting canes (on days when his leg was giving him
trouble), Taylor would emerge from his office, always
fresh, easy in manner, enthusiastic, engaging. Our talk
would begin then and conclude a couple of hours later
after a leisurely meal during which he drank gallons of
iced tea, told fascinating stories, and answered questions
about both his work and his literary career of nearly fifty
years. Those conversations were supplemented by talks
over the telephone after Taylor left Athens, primarily
about his novel *A Summons to Memphis*.

PART ONE

Student: How important do you think a formal education is to a
writer?

Taylor: Every bit of education is invaluable. My teachers believed
in classicism. I took Latin all through high school. It was invaluable
not only for the literature itself but for understanding the English
language. And studying things you don't like is good for young
people. I wish I'd gotten a broader education. I avoided math and
physics in college. Creative writers often are not good in the sciences.

115

But all kinds of knowledge are of value to a writer. I didn't want to write poetry, but my teachers and classmates looked down on fiction; I had to read and write poetry because I had vanity. I learned from trying to do that.

And teaching is good for you. When I started out, I taught freshman English at eight and nine and sophomore lit. at ten. You have to know something to teach. I learned from doing that. I didn't like satire (Swift), but I had to teach it, and I learned to value it.

A gifted person, though, will get an education anywhere.

Student: What about Faulkner's lack of education?

Taylor: He is a great writer, one of my favorites, but his writing often shows that he had little formal education, just as Thomas Hardy didn't. Hardy will misuse words and bend over backwards to bring in classical references, as Ford Madox Ford points out; and so does Faulkner. Faulkner often uses language in an uneducated way. Many learned people are not one-hundredth the writer Faulkner is, but they don't make mistakes like that.

Faulkner didn't really like people at the University of Virginia—his only good friend was the horse trainer. He felt his gaps around academic people. When people asked, "What are you reading, Mr. Faulkner?" he'd say, "Virgil, Homer"—list the greats.

Flannery O'Connor had not read widely when I knew her, but she didn't care. She was once in a forum, and someone asked, "What do you think of Flaubert?" She said, "Haven't read 'im"—and the tone said, "and don't mean to."

McAlexander: Who was your best teacher?

Taylor: Tate. He was the best lecturer; he made literature seem serious, and he had a wonderful personality. He made literature and ideas seem more important than anything else in the world, and you wanted to put everything aside and follow him. He also had a body of ideas that he made very clear.

Student: What about Ransom?

Taylor: He spoke of other professors as evangelical. *He* was very reserved, and that made his wisdom more valuable. He never prepared for class—just read some from the text and talked about how he responded to it. You could sit there and watch him thinking. He was one of the most honest men in the world. He was marvelous for the best students; the others couldn't understand. In later years a student told me, "Now he's senile"; but he was just the same, taking ten matches to light his pipe, and so forth. But his judgment was honest, and he had the educational background. Following him to Kenyon was the best decision I ever made.

Student: How do you explain the phenomenon of so many literary people together at Vanderbilt in the 1920s and 1930s?

Taylor: That happens every so often. Of course the South and its customs had been humiliated by the industrial giant to the north, and Southerners wanted to assert their identity and virtues—like Ireland with England or Poland with Russia—all on the border of a great power. Rebellion holds them together. And the Southern movement took place in the "transmontane" South because that part, the newer part, felt more the need to assert itself as people with education and cultivation.

Student: Are you an Agrarian?

Taylor: I'm not an Agrarian. I did have that kind of background. In my first theme in Allen Tate's freshman English class, I quoted from a speech made by my grandfather: "There is no New South, only the Old South resurrected with the nail prints still in her hands." My family had lived in the country and in the city. But in our household, the country was good, and the city was bad; we never made fun of our old-fashioned country relations. Tate and Ransom reinforced those attitudes. There is a lot of truth in them.

But it was more clearly conceivable to hold Agrarian ideas when I was young. After the 1930s, when the industrialization of the South really began, it seemed impossible to protect it. I'm not political by nature. I began to go along with Agrarian ideas, but at the same time to see the folly of them. I had realized earlier that I could never be a lawyer because I could always see both sides.

And intelligent people that I knew were no longer part of the movement. My father—who felt close to kin and the old order, who would talk this way and argue about it—moved to Southern cities, and when he died, we found that he had sold all his land and put everything into stocks and bonds. He knew where the money was. And one does have to live in the world that he actually inhabits.

Student: Did Randall Jarrell's split with the Agrarians influence you?

Taylor: He was opposed to Agrarianism from the beginning, and he was sometimes really rude to Ransom, but that was his way of rejecting. He influenced me, and I took some of his views as opposed to Tate's.

Student: How did your association with Tate and Ransom affect your writing?

Taylor: The best thing a teacher does is encourage your virtues. I was lucky that first-rate writers with ideas about style and morality, who had grown up as I had, encouraged me. Also you see how they use material. Imitation is the best way to learn—and you disregard things that are not useful to you. Imitation often helps you to learn structure.

Of my own students, I often find that I remember not those who seemed so obviously talented at first, but the ones with grim determination, who studied and learned technique. Often young writers produce something wonderful through instinct, but they don't learn technique, and they don't improve. You have to learn technique consciously. Joyce worked so, but he didn't have the natural gift of Lawrence.

But after you accept and learn from someone, then you must reject him and express your own ideas.

Student: Whom have you rejected?

Taylor: Henry James. As an undergraduate I read him like the Bible. I would read *Wings of the Dove* out loud to Robert Lowell, and he would walk out of the room. But James' experience of life is so different from mine. I was for a time also under Hemingway's influence and then turned against it. I always return to James, though. Often I read him to get myself started writing again. Recently I read a James story that I had never encountered before, "Glasses." It's a very good story.

McAlexander: Is Chekhov as important an influence on you as James?

Taylor: He is different. He came at a later time. My early stories were more moralistic. Chekhov influenced me to try to see things from all sides, to examine things from all sides.

McAlexander: What about Trollope?

Taylor: Oh, I read him for fun. My wife and I have been reading him aloud this winter. He's very good, but I don't think that he's a great writer. One reason is that the minor characters are often wonderful, and the parts on the church and politics are interesting, but he has no intelligent, serious central characters. They don't really engage your interest.

McAlexander: What story do you consider your best?

Taylor: My last story is my best story. I have to feel that way. I hope to get out a book of stories for college reading—"The Old Forest," "In the Miro District," "Miss Leonora," "Venus, Cupid, Folly and Time"—my most ambitious stories.

McAlexander: "Dean of Men"?

Taylor: "Dean of Men" is not one of my favorites; the context is not as interesting.

Student: To what extent is "Dean of Men" autobiographical?

Taylor: Flaubert says, "Madame Bovary, c'est moi." How can you write fiction if you can't imagine it? And how can you imagine it if you don't link your psychology to your characters? Writing starts wth events and experiences that worry me, and I put them together. You write a story in which you are the protagonist, but you have to change him for the theme's sake. It is true that my father's business partner betrayed him, and that my grandfather was betrayed in a Senate race and "died of a broken heart," according to the family story.

McAlexander: How far are we to trust the narrator? How ironically are we to view him?

Student: Is he justifying his life to his son?

Taylor: Yes, he needs to tell the story. The son will not profit from it; his father has sold out to become Dean. . . . My narrators are seldom completely reliable, but they aren't totally unreliable. I sympathize with the narrator; he had a hard time. He's like the graduate students I'd known, with such hard lives that their marriages often didn't last. It's difficult to convey effectively the limitations of a narrator. I've just found a way to do that in the novel *(A Summons to Memphis)* that I'm working on.

PART TWO

McAlexander: I often ask my students, as an exercise, to tell me in one word what a story is about. I'm curious to know whether you could do that for "Venus, Cupid, Folly and Time."

Taylor: That's easy. Incest.

McAlexander: Incest?

Taylor: Social Incest. Some people cannot function outside a narrow social group. They especially can't marry outside the group. That kind of limitation can incapacitate them for life; it works in all kinds of ways. The whole story, of course, is almost an allegory.

McAlexander: How did you respond to the two stories that you re-read for my class?

Taylor: I liked "At the Drugstore" much better than I thought I would. I had expected it to seem too much like a theorum, all the most carefully planned symbolic representation. When I finished "1939," I was almost in tears, not really about the story, but about what I based it on. That all came back in a flood of memory.

McAlexander: That story seems to me to capture remarkably the experience of many talented young men at that age.

Taylor: Yes, I guess so, but it all happened. Jarrell said that I might as well have used the real names. And both Jean Stafford and Lowell were furious at first. Whenever my father or any of my relatives had objected to my using them in my stories, Jean and Cal had said, "Oh, you must pay no attention to that!" But when I used *them*, it was another matter. When I re-read the story, I was surprised that I had presented Jean just as I had. During that period she would affect all sorts of things, wear bohemian clothes and sunglasses. That was the way she was then, but I'm surprised that I presented it.

McAlexander: Did you and Robert Lowell really get in a fight on the train back to Kenyon?

Taylor: Yes, the fight really happened, we did lose the car key in the snow, and the boys were cooking in our room when we got back. I did have to rearrange some things; theme, drama, and characters make demands. And of course the shaping of a story is what makes it. The Yeatsian poem was mine; Lowell said that if I'd used one of his, he'd have sued me all the way to the Supreme Court.

McAlexander: How did you come to write the story?

Taylor: At a cocktail party at Kenyon when I was on the faculty, a Mrs. Brown asked me why I didn't write something about my college days there. I went home and wrote that story. It is my only writing experience of that sort.

McAlexander: I am fascinated both by all your real estate ventures, all of the houses that you've owned and lived in, and by the houses in your fiction. When did your interest in architecture begin?

Taylor: When I was just a child. My family was always making trips across Tennessee. My father was from west Tennessee, my mother's family was from east Tennessee, and both branches had lived at different times in Nashville, which is in the middle Division. It was an awful mistake, by the way, to drop those natural Divisions. The three parts of the state are so different from each other. That's one thing that I'm treating in my novel. At any rate, we were constantly traveling back and forth over the state, and I was always interested in the old houses, and I'd ask my parents questions about them. Both of my parents were good story-tellers, and they'd often tell stories about the houses, about the families that had lived in them.

McAlexander: How many houses have you owned?

Taylor: Oh, I don't know. A number. We've lived in several different houses on just one street in Charlottesville, Rugby Road. For a while we owned Faulkner's house, and Lowell kidded me a lot about that. Once I was thinking of buying a house, and I called Eleanor and told her about it. She said that it didn't sound rundown enough. We have enjoyed fixing them up. Sometimes we'll be driving and see one and say, "That's one we saved." But they do take up part of your imaginative life. They do take time away from writing.

The Taylors were all great builders, and my own family moved around a great deal and lived in a number of houses. Two images stick in my mind from my own family's history. Just before my paternal grandfather died and my father decided to leave the little town of Trenton and go to Nashville, my father had chosen a site for a house just outside Trenton. When we went back there later on visits, we'd often go out to the site; trees had been cleared and some of the materials brought there. I remember so well the site and the experience of going there. The other image is from St. Louis. My father was president of an insurance company, and we lived in a huge, grand house on Washington Terrace, three stories and a basement. Then the depression came, and we had to leave that house. I went back years later to visit my sister who lived in St. Louis. The house had been torn down; even the basement was gone. There was just a great hole in the earth. Those two images are haunting— the life that was never to be and the life that could never be again.

McAlexander: There are a number of houses in your fiction that are memorable, the one in "Porte Cochere," for instance. But the one that is perhaps most vividly presented is the grandmother's house, which the boy visits in the summers, in *A Woman of Means*.

Taylor: That's a marvelous house outside Nashville—"Travelers' Rest," the home of John Overton, who was an important figure in Tennessee history, the friend and ally of Andrew Jackson, and one of the founders of Memphis. My father rented it furnished when we first moved to Nashville. And in later years my brother and I paid long summer visits to the Williamses who lived there—Mrs Williams was an Overton. It's a wonderful house. The oldest part is very early and plain. It had been added to over the years, and the floors were on different levels.

McAlexander: Did you base the Dorset residence in "Venus, Cupid, Folly and Time" on a particular house?

Taylor: There were two. There was a house in St. Louis. During the depression the owners removed the top floor and disconnected the bathrooms in order to save on taxes. I was thinking of that house, but the story really takes place in a house in North Carolina that I was in once. During the visit the owner said to me, "Now you're *not* going to write anything about this house, are you?" And I said, "Oh, *no,* sir." Then about ten years later, I started describing it in the story—a writer will use anything! But many things about that house I had to leave out. They didn't suit my purposes, but also readers would not have believed some of them. Like the case that contained valentines from children who later died.

McAlexander: Where did you get other details that you put in, such as Mr. Dorset's stuffing his sweater inside his trousers? What does that suggest?

Taylor: I had a close friend, a fraternity brother, who used to do that, and I thought it was strange. When I was younger, I would put details like that in, just because I liked them. In Memphis during the depression, there were two old ladies who were driven around by their chauffeur to sell figs—the obvious sexual suggestions there. I drew on that. I plotted that story very carefully, and I drew on all sorts of things that I had seen

McAlexander: That story is one of those set in the fictional place

Chatham. Later stories are set in real places, and much of your most recent fiction is set in Memphis. Can you explain that pattern?

Taylor: I chose the name Chatham because several states have towns and counties named for William Pitt, Earl of Chatham.

McAlexander: Chatham in Pittsylvania County, Virginia.

Taylor: And Pittsburgh, Pennsylvania, and Pittsboro, North Carolina, and so on. It seemed like a representative name. But having a fictional city really didn't work. It is much better to use fully a real place. It gives fiction an added dimension.

McAlexander: I find interesting your use of the name Tolliver for the family in some of your St. Louis stories and plays. It's rather close to Taylor.

Taylor: According to one of my aunts, the Taylors were originally Taliaferros [pronounced Tolliver]. She didn't want anyone to think that we had come from someone who made clothes. The choosing of names for characters and places can become a game. In the novel that I'm writing, the family caravan stops, and the servants stand and look off in the distance in the direction of the little town where they were born. I remember that scene so well from a trip that my own family made. We had stopped at Humboldt, Tennessee. But I didn't want to use the real place name in the novel, and suddenly I thought of the name Huxley, another nineteenth-century scientist.

Back to the houses for a minute. I've also used a couple of houses at Monteagle in my work. A cottage that we owned is the house I had in mind for my play *A Stand in the Mountains.*

McAlexander: I think that play may be the best thing that you've ever written.

Taylor: Yes, I do too.

McAlexander; It's one of the most complex in its presentation of the battle of the sexes.

Taylor: It's been interesting how different people have viewed that. In one production of the play, for instance, the women were emphasized; another production emphasized the men.

McAlexander: That play has never received the attention that it deserves. But you're getting a lot of recognition now after the publication of *The Old Forest and Other Stories.*

Taylor: Yes. My son called the other night, and he said that he wished all of this recognition had come to me years ago. But I said no, better for it to come now. When you're younger, you have a wider range of pleasures and experiences. As you get older, the range diminishes. It is more difficult to have new experiences. So it is much better for me to be getting the attention now.

McAlexander: One pleasure that you've obviously enjoyed for a long time is the friendship of some of the truly important literary people of your time. You told the class that Allen Tate was your best teacher. Did he help you most?

Taylor: Well, it was very important to a young writer to study under a person of Mr. Ransom's authority. And Red Warren has as sweet a nature as anyone I know, and he has been so generous to other writers. He's been so generous in his support of younger writers. Tate did many things for me. He is responsible for my going to Vanderbilt to study under Ransom; he introduced me to Eleanor; he arranged a job for me with a New York publisher after I was discharged from the army. I will always be very grateful to him. Tate was a fascinating person, a person of great charm. And he could be so dramatic. Once while he was divorced, we were together in Nashville, and he became convinced that the brothers of a girl were coming to get him. He insisted that we arm ourselves. He made the entire evening one of great drama.

He was very attractive to women, and he fell very much under the influence of his wives. When he was married to Caroline Gordon, he read the biographies of Confederate generals; with his last wife, it was the lives of the saints; and with his second wife, he was always talking about avant-garde literary figures.

But Tate was interested in everything and in everyone; he loved gossip. When he came to visit us in Columbus, Ohio, he would want us to tell him about everyone there—all the neighbors, the postman, everyone. He was also a great manipulator; he was always telling various ones of us, "Now this is what you must do"—some scheme to advance ourselves in the literary world.

McAlexander: Didn't he get rather crotchety in later life?

Taylor: He quarreled with many old friends. We were estranged for a time over something that he had done. Toward the end I was at Sewanee, and he sent word that he very much wanted to see

Eleanor and me. He had terrible emphysema, and he was weak. The tank of oxygen was in the room. He was supposed to have only a certain amount each day. But it was a wonderful visit. He loved talking, and he talked so well. After we had talked for a while about our own writing and literary matters, he said, "Now, that's enough of that"—he wanted to gossip about people. All the time he would sneak trips to the oxygen tank while listening for his wife's car in the drive. He didn't want to get caught. But the oxygen gave him a kind of high. You would have liked him.

McAlexander: Ransom was quite different from Tate.

Taylor: Mr. Ransom was reserved. His dress and manner reminded you of a preacher. He was like a father to all of us; we wanted his respect. And Lowell was the favorite son.

Eleanor and I very much enjoyed the Ransoms when I taught at Kenyon. The four of us played bridge regularly, the men against the women, and we kept score on a closet door for years. A few times we all wrote poems and read them, impromptu poems. His all came out in his idiosyncratic manner; he would just sit there and write them in that strange style. It was fascinating to watch. And he never realized how unusual they were.

Mrs. Ransom was quite strong-minded and independent—their granddaughter Robb Dew, who is a novelist, has recently written a very good reminiscence of her grandparents. Once when we were living in Columbus, Ohio, Mrs. Ransom drove over from Gambier and spent an evening with us while she was waiting to meet Mr. Ransom's plane. I followed her out to the airport, and we found that the plane had been delayed for several hours, until two or three in the morning. She sent me to the counter with a note to be delivered to him. I had to peek at it. It said something like "Get home the best way you can"!

Another time they were on a trip and stopped at a filling station. Mr. Ransom got the gas, and then he drove off while Mrs. Ransom was still in the bathroom. She flagged down another car—maybe a highway patrolman—and they chased him and ran him down. Mr. Ransom had never noticed that she was missing. He was thinking about something else.

McAlexander: I want to ask you about a pattern that I see in several of your stories. Do you think that Aunt Munsie in "What You Hear From 'Em," the grandfather in "In the Miro District," and Miss Leonora all meet similar fates and for the same reasons?

Taylor: They are all defeated by their cultures. Their cultures have changed, and the change has denied them their old roles. They are defeated and forced to take the only roles available to them. Miss Leonora has been rejected. The old spinster is no longer appreciated as the vessel that transmits the values of education, of civilization— there were so many old ladies in the South like that at one time. She is heroic up to a point; remember that she gives the little black boy the book. But she is finally displaced.

Different times are better for different people. Sam Houston lived at the right time for him—that frontier period when a person could simply leave, disappear, and go to another place to begin anew and make his destiny. It would have been an awful period for me. I could not have stood the isolation.

McAlexander: The three old ladies in "Their Losses" are similarly displaced.

Taylor: Yes, and the real heroine there, in a way, is Cornelia, the one who has moved to Memphis and married the Jew, the one who accepts the world as it is and makes the best of it.

McAlexander: Now to the subject of your novel. You have worked on it for a long time.

Taylor: I kept rewriting and then going over it and making more changes. But now it's the novel that I wanted it to be.

McAlexander: Wasn't the title *Vengeance Is Mine* at one time?

Taylor: Briefly. Then I changed it back to *A Summons to Memphis.*

McAlexander: What other kinds of changes?

Taylor: I tried telling a part of the story from the point of view of Alex Mercer, Phillip Carver's friend. But that didn't work. The whole story had to come from Phillip. What is important is his point of view and the way he goes back and forth over the years trying to understand.

McAlexander: I was compelled to keep reading the galleys, for half the length of the novel without a break, just to find out whether the narrator would answer the summons to come home. That's the same sort of strategy you use in "The Old Forest." There the reader simply *must* know whether Lee Ann is found.

Taylor: That's my version of the cliffhanger (laughs). My early works had no suspense. I came to see the value of it later. It is a good way to get a sense of motion in the work. Fitzgerald is good at that— although there are a number of his works that I don't admire very much. The best are the Basil stories and "The Diamond As Big As the Ritz."

McAlexander: Why doesn't Alex Mercer say good-bye to Mr. Carver after the scene in which the children are keeping the father from visiting Lewis Shackelford?

Taylor: Alex doesn't say good-bye to anyone, but the father notices only Alex's treatment of him. Alex has had enough of all of them.

McAlexander: How is the reader to respond to Holly's view that the harm parents do children must be totally forgiven?

Taylor: I use Holly as a comparative figure to the narrator. Her view is one way of looking at the situation. But she goes too far, and that is not the narrator's final judgment. But after all, how successful are we ever in understanding what has happened to us? That's what I want to suggest in the novel.

McAlexander: At first I felt that the narrator's father was simply a monster. But there is another side to that family history. The children should have resisted, and they were too weak.

Taylor: The narrator is much too *serene*.

McAlexander: Not "alive enough to have the strength to die"? What is the source of that passage in your closing lines?

Taylor: Hardy's poem "Neutral Tones."

McAlexander: What are you working on now?

Taylor: A novel called *To the Lost State,* which is set on a train bringing a senator's body back from Washington for burial in Tennessee. That action takes place in 1915, but the novel goes back and forth in time like *A Summons to Memphis.* The narrator is the senator's grandson, and the most sympathetic character is one of the country relatives on the train, the senator's nephew. The problem that I'm trying to solve at the moment is whether I should let the reader know very clearly just how much the narrator identifies with the country relative. But that's what makes writing fun, working out problems like that.

I'm also writing some sketches of literary people that I've known. And I'm thinking of writing a play about two old widows who have spent most of their lives taking girls to Europe. There is a great deal that I want to do.

Interview: Peter Taylor

W. Hampton Sides/1987

From *Memphis*, 11 (February 1987), 109–117. Copyright ©
1987 by MM Corporation. Reprinted by permission.

Most critics consider the seventy-year-old Peter Taylor to
be one of the masters of the modern American short
story. A native of Tennessee, Taylor is the author of six
books of stories, four books of plays, and two novels. His
stories, which have frequently appeared in *The New
Yorker,* have received numerous literary honors. In 1985,
Taylor won the prestigious PEN/Faulkner Award. A chapter from his most recent novel, *A Summons to Memphis*
(Knopf, $15.95), was first excerpted in the September
issue of this magazine. A few months later, the book was
nominated for the American Book Award, along with
E. L. Doctorow's *World's Fair.* Though Doctorow won the
prize, Taylor created an enormous controversy within
literary circles by his refusal to attend the ceremony after
publicly denouncing the American Book Award nominating process. He argued that by naming several nominees
but picking only one recipient, the judges were, in effect,
setting up winners and losers, thereby creating the impression that writers are in competition with one another.
Since the controversy erupted late last fall, Taylor has
declined to grant personal interviews with national publications.

Much of Taylor's fiction focuses on families, particularly
on aristocratic Tennessee families of several generations
ago, and the ways in which a particular locale shapes the
dynamics of family life. That locale, as often as not, is
Memphis ("Any of Taylor's books will serve you Memphis
on a silver platter," *Esquire* declared in 1985). Of Taylor's
most popular story, a tale of a Memphis debutante en-
titled "The Old Forest," *Washington Post* literary critic
Jonathan Yardley once wrote: "By comparison, almost
everything else published by American writers in recent
years seems small, cramped, brittle, inconsequential;

among American writers now living only Eudora Welty has accomplished a body of fiction so rich, durable, and accessible as Taylor's."

Born in [1917], Taylor grew up in Nashville, St. Louis, and Memphis, and studied at Kenyon College and Southwestern at Memphis (now Rhodes College). He has taught literature at a number of universities, including Harvard, the University of North Carolina, and Memphis State University. Since 1967, he has been a Commonwealth Professor of English at the University of Virginia. Though he is now recovering from a stroke he suffered last summer, Taylor is still at work on a new novel and several short stories. This interview was conducted in Charlottesville, Virginia, where Taylor lives with his wife, poet Eleanor Ross Taylor

Memphis: You managed to create quite a stir over the American Book Award back in the fall. Any misgivings?

Taylor: It was an absurd thing to do, I guess. But on the other hand, I think it is making the writer look ridiculous to have a number of people nominated with only one winner. I just didn't want to get up on a platform and be told, "You're good, but you're not as good as Doctorow." It's shallow treatment of people. They just ought to announce the winner for each category, and only one winner, like the Pulitzer. I wanted it understood that I think all competitions between writers are invidious. They create bad feelings. It's treating a literary event like an athletic event or a Hollywood event.

Memphis: I guess most people would share your view on this. What puzzled so many people in the literary world, though, was your timing. Why did you wait until after you had learned you wouldn't be receiving the award to criticize the nominating process?

Taylor: You see, I wouldn't have had the chance to speak my mind at that group meeting, because only the winners are asked to speak. And so this way, by publicly turning down the second prize, I thought I might at least have some influence. I wanted to have an effect on the American Book Award people to stop running a race among writers. I don't take a high or lofty tone about it. It's just a practical thing, a matter of good taste and good sense not to treat writers that way.

Memphis: American Book Award or not, *A Summons to*

Memphis has sold well and been extremely well received by the critics. What struck me most about the novel was the way you juxtaposed life in two different cities in Tennessee, Nashville and Memphis, and made those two places seem worlds apart, almost as if they had been two different countries. You talk in great detail about such things as the definitive Nashville suit, the trademark Memphis hat, the innumerable differences in accent and style and attitude. It occurred to me that today, with all the interstates and shopping malls and glass towers of suburbia, you'd be hard-pressed to make the same kinds of sharp contrasts between those two places. We're getting more alike, it seems.

Taylor: All places get more and more alike, of course. But there will always be subtle differences to be seen if you watch for them. Now, when I was a boy living in Memphis, I wouldn't have been able to pinpoint all those differences between life in Nashville and life in Memphis. It's looking back on it that makes you see them. And then, too, in writing a book like *A Summons to Memphis,* I was probably more sensitive than normal to these differences. I exaggerated them for my interest and for the sake of the book.

Memphis: We are always hearing the cliché about how Southerners are supposed to have a strong sense of place, but in so many of your stories, the sense of place is truly pivotal.

Taylor: I think the business of a novelist is to make the differences between places seem significant. So when you get to writing about "place" in fiction, you want to make that place seem as distinctive as you can. You use the paraphernalia of life—the local color—to make the story seem real. As I was writing *A Summons to Memphis,* I had a lot of fun seeing how much I could get into the contrasts between two different places, and then making the story be one that made use of those contrasts.

Memphis: In the novel, you suggested that not only was Memphis vastly different from Nashville, but it was different in such a way that moving there irrevocably changed the lives of the protagonist and his family. And I understand that much of the book was autobiographical.

Taylor: Well, I knew how tremendously different our family life was after we moved to Memphis. First of all, it was simply an uprooting experience leaving [St. Louis], especially for me, because I was 15 then. It would be hard for anybody at the age of 15 to pick up and go somewhere else. That's when you're first interested in girls, cigarettes, life. And then, too, my family had many, many ties in Nashville. So in the book I tried to look back at these two lives, and rather than seeing how alike Memphis and Nashville were, I tried to see how they were different and why it might be significant in the lives of my characters.

Memphis: And what are—were—those differences?

Taylor: Of course, Memphis is in the deep South, while Nashville tends to look eastward. My mother always used to complain that Memphis was really a part of Mississippi, and that the newspapers had all Mississippi news and Arkansas news and not enough Tennessee news. And historically, Memphis and Nashville have grown up very differently, against the backdrop of two very different agricultural pursuits. Memphis was always a cotton town, and the wealth was concentrated in those circles, while the agricultural economy around Nashville was, to a large extent, livestock—cattle and horses.

Memphis: Throughout the book you were arriving at all kinds of odd and colorful distinctions.

Taylor: I said somewhere in the book that the "high society" people in Memphis tended often to go to Marshall Field's in Chicago to shop, while the people in Nashville would go to New York. The pull was in a different direction, you see. I like to try to reach some kind of generalization like that, to build up to it. I think it's a very good trait to argue from the particular to the general. You find it in all literature. You can find it in Proust, you find it in Tolstoy, and all the great people.

Memphis: It does seem a very Southern characteristic to dwell on these kinds of contrasts between places, contrasts which the casual observer—or the outsider—might never notice.

Taylor: I once stopped at a service station in Kentucky, and there was a man who was telling me how differently the people talked over in the next county, how "Southern" they were. Just one county over. Of course, he didn't think his county was Southern at all. Well, you see, it's all in the eye of the beholder.

Memphis: That same phenomenon, of exaggerating the differences between your home and the rest of the world, runs through a great deal of Southern literature. It's the search for Southern identity or something such as that.

Taylor: And in a very real way, that's what great literature consists of: discovering what your life is like and why it's the way that it is. It's the way that the Irish have developed a great literature. Because here is this enormous British Empire right next to them. So the Irish have all been trying to assert their individuality. They want to say what it's like to be a Dubliner or what have you. The same is true of the South. Edmund Wilson said the South was like a little Balkan state on the edge of a big and powerful empire. The South has always been trying to identify what it was about itself that was different from other parts of the country.

Memphis: But you write about the South from the perspective of a person who has lived outside the South a great deal, traveling and teaching and studying all over the country.

Taylor: A person whose point of view I like immensely is Robert Penn Warren—and maybe I've been influenced a lot by him. He's a Southerner to the last ditch, and yet he's one of the most liberal human beings in the world. He loves the South and yet he criticizes it as he pleases.

One of the reasons I found myself so interested in the South was that I lived out of South a lot when I was a boy in St. Louis, and later, at Kenyon College in Ohio. Nothing makes you a Southerner more than living out of the South. In school in St. Louis, my brother and I were teased a lot about our Southern accent. I was always made aware of my roots going back to Tennessee. I didn't stand a chance of forgetting any of that when I was growing up.

Memphis: Writing as you so often do about aristocratic families in the South, one of the characters that consistently crops up in your stories is the black servant—the maid, the nurse, the chauffeur. The relationship between white families and their black servants has always seemed to play an important role in Southern literature.

Taylor: I have a very good friend named James McPherson who is a wonderful black writer. We used to joke about doing a book together that would be called *Upstairs, Downstairs in the Old South*. You see, his mother was a maid and cook in Savannah, and he knew about racial relations from that angle. And, of course, I knew the other angle.

In the Twenties, we had four black servants. They were all from the same county in Tennessee where my father's home was, and, as it happened, they were also named "Taylor." And sometimes we'd even go so far as to pretend that we were all directly related to each other—one big happy family. We were allowed to bring boys home for lunch on Saturday, and I remember the black cook, Lucille Taylor, would come in and tease my brother by calling him "Cousin Bob" right there in front of our white guests because, well, here we all had the same last name. And the other little white boys didn't quite understand. It would infuriate my brother, but the rest of us would always laugh about it.

Memphis: It's possible to idealize certain aspects of those old days when affluent families had lifelong black servants around the home—the closeness, the sense of shared family roots, the possibility for genuine friendships. But it also might be said that this was a paternalistic situation that left blacks no room for improvement.

Taylor: Yes, of course, it was an inherently patronizing situation, and there was no future in it. And it's all over and very different now. But the relationship our family had with our servants was in many ways more human and more real than the relationships that exist today between blacks and whites in a place like Harlem, where the races are completely separated and hatred builds up.

You see, it was altogether different when the servants shared your own name, when they shared the same family history from the same little town in the country. There was a great interplay between blacks and whites in our situation. For example, we had a woman who was called "Mammie" who had been a slave before the Civil War. She had been my father's nurse, and my nurse. I remember she used to tell me little things about my father, things he did when he was a little boy. So there was a great deal of continuity there.

I can't see how, growing up as I did, among the blacks looking after my greatest needs, and even talking to me about such things as poetry—I can't see how one can grow up like this and then not be sympathetic to blacks. How can one be a racist? My feelings were deeper for the black servants than they were for my own mother when I was growing up. And they were so much a part of the family.

Memphis: Your stories often do paint a benign portrait of the racial set-up in the South of several decades ago.

Taylor: There are certainly other Southern writers—like Shelby Foote, for example—who are much more reconstructed than I am, and who are much more liberal in their thought. But in my work, I try to be interested in the human qualities in both blacks and whites and how their humanity sometimes overcomes the barriers that distinguish them. Often a black in my stories has responded by forgiving the whites for all they've done to him. Now, that's an idealist Christian view of things, and maybe an impossible one. But these things that seem so awful in our upbringing—like meanness to blacks—however bad they are, they sometimes help us to identify ourselves. They help us in seeing that there is good and bad in all people.

Memphis: Just as there was some good mixed with the bad of the antebellum South.

Taylor: I don't mean to give a lecture on what the Civil War was about. But the difference between an old agrarian civilization and a new industrial civilization, and the difference in manners of these two ways of life, is a profound one. I of course recognize that any slavery is barbarous. On the other hand, the business of having slaves was terrible not only for the slaves, but for the white Southerners, too. It had a terrible effect on their view of the world. The history of the South drives stupid people to enmity, but it's important to realize that we were all trapped in this historical situation.

Memphis: Not many people grow up in the South today feeling like they're trapped in a historical situation, and fewer still think about having lost a war.

Taylor: No, of course not. It's all an abstraction to your generation. But you see, my grandfather had been a Confederate soldier, and I remember that one of the great occasions when I was growing up was the Confederate Reunion. All those old Confederates would be there. And I vividly remember my uncle as an old man—he had had his hand shot through at Shiloh, and was paralyzed. He had this special fork made to fit on his wrist, and I remember how terrified I was by this awful looking claw of a hand. Well, you see, the war was very real to me.

Memphis: You often write about old affluent Southern families, families that do feel a certain allegiance to that antebellum past.

Taylor: That's the world that I knew growing up, the world of the so-called upper class people. I know everything that was wrong and wretched about them. But, on the other hand, they fascinate me. They represent an attitude toward the past that is terribly important to society. Also, as an author, I recognize that writing about the so-called high society and making it appealing to my readers is a challenge. In "The Old Forest" I deliberately made the heroine a society girl, a debutante, even though all of us might find another character much more admirable—someone who was attractive and went out to nightspots and was loads of fun. But I said to myself, it would be more interesting to see if I can make this society girl appealing as a human being and see what her life is. I wanted to see human beings set in certain historical situations from which they can't escape.

In this case, the character happened to be a girl who realized that the only power that she had was to be a rich married woman in Memphis, and that was all that was offered to her. In too many novels and movies, it's that little girl who's not in the establishment who's the heroine. I wanted to see if I could make that other one appealing. That's part of the power of writing fiction: You can cut through and make a person who's normally unattractive do heroic things despite themselves and their situation.

Interview with Peter Taylor

Barbara Thompson/1987

This interview will be published in *The Paris Review* sometime
in 1987. It appears here with the gracious permission of Barbara
Thompson and the editors of *The Paris Review.*

Peter Taylor is a story teller of fixed abode. His ancestral
ghosts inhabit an irregular triangle formed by Memphis,
Nashville and the farm at Trenton in Gibson County,
where his father grew up and to which in childhood the
family habitually returned.

The power and resilience of his roots have allowed him
a peripatetic life. He and his wife, the poet Eleanor Ross
Taylor, have owned nearly 30 houses since the first small
duplex they bought in 1947 with the Randall Jarrells,
when Taylor and Jarrell were teaching at the Women's
College of the University of North Carolina.

Our conversations over the tape recorder took place, as
well, in many locations. The first was in the spring of 1981
in a dim corner of the Cosmos Club, a stately Victorian
edifice on Massachusetts Avenue in Washington, D.C.,
where Taylor stayed while conducting a week's workshop
at American University. He sat under a larger-than-life
portrait of some long-gone member in a stiff wooden
chair that could only remind him that he too was sitting
for a portrait, rather than enjoying his own or anybody
else's social conversation. He was not, then or ever, fully
reconciled to the idea of a recorded dialogue, an extended self-revelation. "There is something offensive to
me about a man or woman's confessing all to the world. I
never believe a word he or she says, especially when it's
ever so consistent. Always there is that ugly ego ex-
posed. . . . In my own case, how could I possibly assume
that the world would have any interest in what I have to
say about myself and/or my writing? Anybody but a
friend, that is. . . ."

And so we talked "on contingency"—that if at the end
it was too hateful to him, the transcript would go into a

locked drawer. At various times it sat there for a long
time. In the meantime we met and talked a half-dozen
times over the small Sony, in a variety of places. Early on,
in a high-ceilinged room with fresh paint but no furniture
that my husband and I had just bought in mid-Manhat-
tan. We dragged in the kitchen table and sat at the two
small rush-seated chairs until they got too uncomfortable,
then adjourned to the Russian Tea Room catty-corner,
where the tape recorder picked up more of the gossip
from the next table than it did Peter's anyhow off-the-
record stories of being young with Lowell and Jarrell and
Katherine Anne Porter. We talked again that winter in
Key West, Florida, where he and Eleanor wintered in a
white conch house with a deep tree-shaded garden.
There was a party that weekend, the Taylor's customary
mix of local people and old friends, some of whom were
poets and fiction writers like James Merrill, Richard
Wilbur, John Ciardi, James Boatwright. . . .

His house in Charlottesville, Virginia, is the serene
repository of many inheritances: mellow old furniture and
tall family portraits, muted oriental rugs on polished
floors. There is a youthful portrait of Taylor over the
mantelpiece in the library, across from the carved Victorian settee that he and Eleanor were bequeathed by
Jean Stafford (Lowell) Liebling, friend of decades. In his
basement study, books line the walls, floor to ceiling, and
a pair of sofas covered with old Indian handblock cotton
offer comfort for the reader, and a place to sit and talk.
Across the room his antique workdesk stands against the
wall. It has many small drawers, and its writing surface
closes up like a box. On one side a dictionary lies open
on its own table; on the other his seafoam Olivetti man-
ual. At eye-level atop the desk an ornate square clock of
polished burl waits, its glass ajar, to be set and wound.
Everywhere in these rooms one is conscious of the past as
useful, beautiful and suffused with meaning.

Interviewer: Why did you become a writer, a story teller?

Taylor: I think a great part of it was the storytelling in the family. I
was so lucky to come along out of this family of storytellers. My
grandfather was famous for his tales. There used to be cartoons
about him in the Washington papers—standing in the Senate
cloakroom telling stories to the other senators. He was of the

generation just following the Civil War; he was a little boy then. His father was of the war generation. He, that great-grandfather, was a lawyer, a clergyman, a land owner. He went to Princeton and was a Unionist. In fact he was Commissioner of Indian Affairs under the first President Johnson. He was enlightened and freed his slaves.

But his wife was for the Confederacy, more or less. Her brother was a Confederate senator from Tennessee. That's why the younger children of the next generation were afterwards to become Democrats and the older children Republicans. . . . We grew up, in my generation, with political battles at home that were sometimes bloody between those great-uncles and aunts. But I think it did give me a sense of history, a sense of the past. I began to make up stories about these things, the old houses, Robert E. Lee, Southern things that I was obsessed by even then, at eight or nine. And I did have considerable imagination, of course, and so when I began to make up stories about my forbears, I began, you know, to exercise my power over them. *That's* one of the satisfactions of writing fiction!

I think one of the reasons that all of this was so interesting to me was that we lived outside the South, away from what we thought of as the South, and yet there was constant talk at our table about Tennessee, constant plans for going back there at Christmas, at Easter, at every holiday. This was when we lived in St. Louis. We considered that far up north!

Interviewer: And even then you took Tennessee with you.

Taylor: I have always said there are no more loyal Southerners than those who grew up *just* outside the South or in the Border States. We lived in a little South of our own in St. Louis. We had a houseful of servants from my father's farm in the cotton country of West Tennessee, and the adults—black and white—would talk about the South, about the way things used to be there. We had very intelligent people working for us. Lucille, who really ran the house, had been to college for two or three years, and had taught school. That was the tragic thing in those days: even when the Negroes went off to college, there was really nothing they could do with their education—especially during the Depression years—and they would come back home and go into service. Lucille would talk to me about my writing and my efforts to paint. I had more conversations with her than with my mother on those subjects—and of course far more than with my father. Lucille had more influence on me when I was a child than any other adult, unless it were her cousin Basil Manley Taylor, who was our butler. It has always been difficult for me to see how people who grew up in the South, brought up by people like Lucille Taylor and B. M. Taylor, could be guilty of race prejudice. The people that loved me most and that I loved most, I think, when I was growing up were these people.

Interviewer: In the stories they come across as very powerful, those black servants.

Taylor: They were, indeed. My nurse, the Aunt Muncie in "What You Hear from 'Em?" was the same nurse that my father had when he was a baby. She absolutely belonged to us, or we absolutely belonged to her. She often talked to us about having been a slave. She never knew how old she was. The only way we could estimate her age was by remembering she said always that she was "a girl up about the Big House when Freedom came." That meant that she was about twelve years old, the age when she would have gone into her mistress's house as maid, and that was before Emancipation. Mammy adored my father, but she made my mother's life hell. She had run my grandmother's house as long as *she* lived, and when her old mistress died she had to be taken on by my mother. Mother would often send her away because she would take it upon herself to dismiss one of the other servants without so much as consulting Mother. She was jealous of the other maids and would send them packing if they were in too much favor with Mother. One of the crises between her and Mother was over the use of butter plates. Butter plates were a fashion Mother had brought with her from Washington (She and my father had married in Washington when Grandfather was in the Senate.). Mammy said, "Ain't no need in nastyin' up all them dishes." And then when Mother would try to dismiss her, Mammy would say "You *can't* fire me. I was here afore you come here, and I'll be here when you gone." She felt she was the real authority in the house, and of course now that Grandmother was dead my father spoiled her. She was a wonderful character—even Mother recognized that—very tiny, what used to be called a "Guinea nigger." She came to Tennessee, as an infant I think, by way of South Carolina. One time my father's most important client—the richest man in the State—was having dinner at our house. He and my father were talking endlessly over the meal. Mammy was in the kitchen—she ran the kitchen and cooked too. Someone else served at table. And when the meal had gone on too long, she entered through the swinging door and tapped my father on the head with her knuckles, saying, "Quit 'at talkin' and eat them vittles." This to my mother's great embarrassment and to my father's delight.

Interviewer: Your mother was unusually important to you, wasn't she?

Taylor: I was a mama's boy. Not that she made me a mama's boy. She was not that dominating sort of woman. But I adored her from the day I was born, I suppose. I thank God that she rejected my adoration to some extent. She simply wouldn't have it. She was very affectionate but she did not pay me any more attention than she did the other children. When people would say, "Oh, this is your favorite," she would say, "Well, let's say *I'm his* favorite," or something like that. If she had not been that way I think she might have ruined my life, because I think that is often the fate of little boys who adore their mothers. If the mother responds, it's a love affair for life. But my mother wouldn't have it so. She was much too interested in my father. He was the only man in her life. At an early age I had to look around for someone else.

Interviewer: In the dedication to your *Collected Stories* you spoke of her as the best teller of tales you ever knew.

Taylor: She was that. She was constantly pouring out stories. You couldn't stop her. When she got very old she became less critical than formerly. That is, her inhibitions broke down, and she didn't censor her stories to the same degree. We would suddenly discover new things in her stories that had been suppressed before. A shocking love affair or a divorce—I mean, that is, the *reason* for the divorce or the *real* nature of the love affair had been suppressed. . . .

She would tell a story over and over again, and she would tell it in precisely the same words every time. My Father would do that too. And she would begin by saying, "Have I told you about the time. . . ." Since one had heard it about twenty times, one would say, "Yes, Mother, you have." And she would proceed to tell it again.

Interviewer: Many of the early stories are in a woman's voice or from her point of view.

Taylor: When I first began writing stories, I wrote about Blacks a

great deal, and I wrote about women. I didn't begin with any
conscious philosophy, but I had a store of stories that I knew, that I
had been told, and I felt I had to write them. And I discovered in
writing them that certain people were always getting the short end. I
found the Blacks being exploited by white women, and the white
women being exploited by the white men. In my stories that always
came through to me and from the stories themselves I began to
understand what I really thought.

Interviewer: Lawrence's saying: "Trust the tale not the teller!"

Taylor: I quote Frank O'Connor to my students—What he said
about Joyce: that when you are writing a story, at some point the
story must take over. You are not going to be able to control it. I think
this is true. O'Connor says he thinks Joyce controls his stories too
tightly—"Who ever heard of a Joyce story taking over?" he asks—
and that there is a deadness about them. You have got to keep the
story opened up, let the story take over at some point.

Interviewer: Do you always know the ending when you begin?

Taylor: I know one ending. But before I've worked on a story very
long I know another. That's part of the fun of it. You begin with one
thing, but the story itself may change your mind by the end. I always
have some idea, but I think it's important to keep your story free
when you are writing it, rather than working mechanically towards a
fixed ending. I often reverse my understanding in the course of
writing a story. Perhaps my real feelings come out as I write.

Interviewer: In ways you hadn't imagined?

Taylor: That happens to me more often than not. I didn't know
what was going to happen in "The Old Forest." I didn't plan all the
business of the hunt for Lee Ann or understand its significance. The
significance began to emerge as I was writing it, and my true feelings
about the characters began to emerge. The story came from something I remembered. I did have such an accident in the family car,
and there were some incidents and characters like those I describe. . . . There was a girl like Lee Ann and there was another set of
young people that I sometimes ran with, and the accident occurred a
few blocks from where she lived, and she was involved in it. But it
was only after I began writing the story that I realized the significance
of that girl. And obviously it was too carefully plotted, at last, to have
happened that way.

Then there was another story of mine called "Guests," an earlier
one, about a family who have cousins visiting them from the country.
I hadn't planned for anyone to die when I was writing at the
beginning of the story, but then it suddenly seemed the only way the
story *could* end.

Interviewer: What do you begin with, in those cases where it isn't
a remembered event or an old family tale? The kernel of the story.

Taylor: I often begin with a character or a situation I've observed
or even with a joke I've heard. Often a very serious story has begun
with a joke. If a joke or anecdote sticks in my mind for years, I know
there must be something in it that means something to me that I am
not conscious of. This is what I mean when I say I feel one learns
about oneself from writing fiction. If a story has stuck with me for
years, even a dirty story, a dirty joke, I'll think the story must contain
some profound meaning for me and about me. . . .

I'll give you an example. There's a story called "Heads of Houses."
Well, ten years before I wrote it I knew a couple who went to stay in
the summer with the wife's parents up in the mountains of Tennessee.
The two couples got on each other's nerves terribly. Their summer
together was a disaster, more or less, and so the young husband
pretended he had received a telegram or letter—I think this got into
the story—calling him back to the university where he taught. And
when they set out for home and were driving down the mountain-
side, they saw the father and mother and bachelor brother join hands
and dance in a circle on the lawn—they were so glad the young
couple had gone! And, you understand, the young couple had been
feeling guilty about leaving.

When I began the story, the very point of it was to be that dancing
on the lawn. That's what had originally appealed to me. But when I
finished it, it was all wrong. When I saw how wrong it was, I tore up
the story without ever looking at it again. And then I wrote it again
from scratch—in quite a different form. When I wrote it the first time,
it was the story of the two couples, and in the background was a
brother, one who danced with the parents in a circle as the young
couple departed. That was really his only role. But by the time I got
the story worked out the second time, I saw how he was really the
most sympathetic character in it. Everyone else is enjoying (or
suffering) a rich family life, but the old bachelor brother is not having

any life at all. And by the time I finished the second version there wasn't even any dancing on the lawn. The parents and the brother . . . are too preoccupied with the significance of the moment. The brother simply stands there juggling apples. And so the important image I began with never got into the story at all.

Then there is a story called "The Hand of Emmagene," about a girl who cuts off her hand. Well, I'd heard that story fifteen years before, at least. It was told to me by the same woman, Lucy Hooke, who told me the story of "Heads of Houses." She was a marvelous story teller—you know how some people have a great talent for telling a story but can't write one. Just as many writers can't actually *tell* a story. Well, Lucy Hooke told me about the severed hand. It was her brother who found it, I think. It was a young woman's hand. Why had she done it? What had happened? In real life she was a girl from East Tennessee, which is generally considered the puritanical part of the state, up-country. Nobody knew why she cut off her hand. That's the mystery we were left with. I only knew that I must imagine why some young woman would do such a thing, what it signified. But I didn't know how to use it, or what it meant to me, and how I would fit something like that into the quiet world of the stories I usually write. And then at last I realized that what I had to do to dramatize it, was to put it against the background of the most conventional people I could think of, just perfectly plain and unimaginative people. And in dramatizing it I found its significance. That was at least twenty-five years after the event.

I have another story called "Her Need." I have rewritten it since *In the Miro District* appeared. The story came out of—well, I was walking early one morning in Charlottesville and saw a young woman, thirty-five or so, with her teen-age son beside her in her car, as she sped along through the residential streets, driving him some-where. And I began to speculate upon what they were doing, where they were going. I went home and wrote the story that day.

Sometimes you have a story that's been in your mind a long time. I have one story that I haven't written yet that I want to write. I recently thought about it again when we were reading Trollope's *Barchester Towers*. I want to bring out the story of the people who leave a town, leave the world they have always lived in and go off and become something else. What reminded me of it was the Stanhopes in

Trollope. They were the people who had been off in Italy and then came back to Barchester. They are very Continental, all their manners are different, and they are rather resented and thought odd by everybody. It's a big part of the novel.

Well, I have seen that happen. These people would go off and become very rich someplace else, and often they would come back to Nashville or Memphis or St. Louis. And they weren't quite accepted. I don't know quite what it means: these people all wanted to be rich themselves, but if somebody went off and got to be president of U.S. Steel or owned it or something, people back home rather rejected them.

I'll get some little theme like that and go over it and over it and wonder why it interests me and what there is in it. . . . Ask myself where does that lead and what does it signify? And is this just a frivolous interest or a profound one? What is marvelous is when your frivolous interests (your interests in the world, just representing it and imitating life) coincide with some serious theme that you are concerned with and some serious feelings. When the two coincide, that's what's marvelous and fun.

But sometimes a story stays in your mind for a long time and refuses to yield the significance it has for you. It's like trying to discover what your dreams mean.

Interviewer: When did you know that you were going to be a writer?

Taylor: When I finished school I received a scholarship to Columbia University. But it didn't cover all my expenses and my father was dead set against my accepting it. It created a great crisis in the family. My mother was all for my going (for my doing whatever I chose to do). She went out to the stores and outfitted me, even packed the wardrobe trunk. But my father held out against it. He was determined that I should go to Vanderbilt, where he had gone to college. I was equally determined that I shouldn't go to Vanderbilt. So, instead, I went out to Southwestern there in Memphis and took some courses and at the same time got work at the newspaper. I was only taking courses as a special student. It was cheaper that way, I believe.

And that was the greatest piece of good luck for me, because there in Tennessee during the Depression some of the best writers in the country (or in the English-speaking world) were teaching: Allen Tate,

John Crowe Ransom, Robert Penn Warren. I knew all those people when I was very young. Also Katherine Anne Porter and Andrew Lytle. Allen Tate particularly made a great impression on me. I had him as a freshman English instructor, at Southwestern, and he was electrifying. He talked about the *art* of fiction, taking it seriously as a form. It was his genius as a teacher that he made young people feel the importance of literature, the importance of art. That came just at the right moment for me. I had already realized that I had a welter of stories I wished to tell. I had written stories, I had written poems, but I had no real principles of writing, but when I became interested in the formal qualities, art and life itself meant something. I really don't know what I thought about up until that time. Later in life, Allen Tate and I quarrelled. I think he did me a great injury. But I was able to forgive him because that injury counted for almost nothing compared to what he taught me when I was young.

The next summer I took a writing course with Tate, in fiction, and that was the real beginning. It was a very fortunate thing for me. Allen liked my stories immensely. He wrote letters to Robert Penn Warren about them—at that time Warren and Cleanth Brooks were editing *The Southern Review*—and sent him two of my stories, without my knowledge. That was very like Tate. He was ever generous with young people, to the end of his life. I know he sent those stories because in Warren's preface to my first book he mentions that he had rejected them and expresses regret for having done so. Actually it was very wise of him, and I am grateful to him for it now. But I am grateful to him for so many, many things. One can't have a better friend than Robert Penn Warren, or a more delightful companion.

I saw that first story just the other day, in an old copy of a magazine called *River.* When Warren didn't take those stories, I sent them to a man who'd written to me from Oxford, Mississippi. His magazine ran just a few issues, but my first story and Eudora Welty's first story were in that issue.

Interviewer: What came next?

Taylor: Allen Tate persuaded me I should go that next year to Vanderbilt. At Vanderbilt, I met John Crowe Ransom. He was a great poet. One never doubted that. But you never got to know him well—that is, not when you were a student. Later on we became good friends, played bridge together every week for years, but not in the early days. He was very different from Tate, who dramatized everything, even his friendships with students. Ransom's way was the opposite. He was all understatement. You would go to his office for a conference on a story, would bring the story for him to read, and he would say almost nothing. What he would say was very much to the point and counted a great deal with me, but you had to prod him, pull it out and listen carefully. He had pertinent things to say, but he hated what he sometimes called "evangelical teaching."

Ransom was a disciplinarian in his way and was narrow in his way. He had but little interest in fiction, and he tried his best to persuade me to write poetry. I remember I wrote a story in which I included a little poem. The poem was necessary to the story, I believe. I kept that paper for years because he wrote on it *"B* for the story, *A* for the little poem." That was his way of pressing me to write poetry. And I have to say that Mr. Ransom prevailed, because the first thing I ever published was a poem, the year I graduated from Kenyon.

He was the best kind of teacher or the best for me at that time. He was a satisfying, reassuring person to talk to about one's work just because he *was* so impersonal. When you gave him a poem to read, the first thing he did was to look at the poem and tap on the desk to make sure the meter was correct. Then he carefully checked the rhyme scheme. He would not discuss other elements of the poem until he had done that.

It seems now that what he taught me about writing was compression. And compression is what I have set great store by as a short story writer. He was so questioning of every detail in the manuscript before him that you felt compelled to make everything functional and to be ready to defend it. I think that habit carried over into story writing, for me. I believe that's one reason I write stories instead of novels. As Faulkner is said to have said, Everyone wants to write poetry in the beginning but if you can't write poetry you write short stories, and if you can't write short stories you write novels. Well, that's too easy, but still there is some truth in it.

And of course when I was at Kenyon I was writing poems in self-defense. The general interest there at that time was all in poetry, not at all in fiction. I refer to Mr. Ransom's interest of course, but it must be remembered I was rooming with Robert Lowell. And Randall

Jarrell was there, too. Randall knew a great deal about fiction, but his chief concern was with poetry of course.

Interviewer: Was Jarrell an important influence?

Taylor: He had tremendous influence on me for several years, most of all on my reading. I think I began reading Chekhov under his influence back at Vanderbilt, but I'm not sure. He was the first serious literary person I knew who read Chekhov stories and could talk about them. Other people would tell you they read Chekhov or admired Chekhov, but they didn't really know his stories. Very few people have read them even now. I think it's because his stories have the compression of poetry. Most readers don't know how he is to be read. He gives the illusion of course that he is just telling a simple tale. Readers often feel it's not much of a tale, that "nothing happens." But actually every line is *packed*. I don't know how much I have been influenced by him. I don't ever consciously think, "Ah, this is a Chekhov effect!" But it is bound to affect one, anything you admire so much. Without knowing it, you are going to steal from it, or be influenced by its subtle structure and statement. That's one reason for a young writer to read a master.

But one goes through phases, I think. Most people do. Everybody should. After Chekhov it was James for me. Since Jarrell didn't like James' fiction, it became one of our great subjects for debate. He would make condescending remarks about James, say really silly things and bend double with laughter. And so finally we got so we avoided the subject. I went through a period when I read nothing but James. Lowell and I tried to read *The Golden Bowl* aloud! It is very hard to do. I suppose I absorbed something from Chekhov—people have pointed out evidence of it in my work, Jarrell especially did— but James I *consciously* learned from. I imitated him. And then I had to unlearn some of it. I think it is good to imitate for a time, but then you have to discard what you can't use. In the long run, a good writer doesn't have to worry about stealing or borrowing. What he can make his own he will keep without giving it a thought. What he can't he will discard.

Interviewer: Which were the Jamesian stories?

Taylor: I'm almost afraid to say, for fear that it doesn't show in the least. "A Spinster's Tale" would certainly be one, although other people may not see it. I was experimenting in those days in different ways. One of my ghost plays seems a direct steal from "The Jolly Corner," but I didn't realize it until I had almost finished writing it. It is the one where a man comes back to St. Louis to see his old girl friend and comes upon himself as he might have been had he married that girl. It is perilously near "The Jolly Corner."

Then I had a Lawrence period. I still consider Lawrence's short stories the greatest stories of this century. I keep going back to them. The feeling for nature in them is quite wonderful. It is rather the opposite of James. That is one of the things Jarrell would say about James, that in all of James you could never imagine finding a description of a landscape. I have dug out a few. But there are not many.

One must learn from the masters and one must learn from one's contemporaries. There is nothing that can take the place of that. I think what young writers profit most from in their association with older writers is from the opportunity it gives them to observe those writers' attitude toward their own work and toward literature. That's the great thing when you are young and trying to discover where your own talent lies. Knowing Tate and Ransom at a very young age, and Warren somewhat later, opened it all up to me. They related art to life for me and made me understand what I wished to do with my life.

At that time I was learning craft and art. Craft has come to have a bad connotation. Writing is *not* a craft, it's an art. Or, rather, it is not *just* a craft. But there is a craft element in it, and that's the easiest thing to talk about. As a teacher I talk about craft because it is one way of getting into talking about writing with students. I don't believe in talking too much about the subject or the personal life of the writer. You can talk endlessly about character and that sort of thing, but it can be just as interesting talking about a bad story as talking about a brilliant one if you have not read either of them!

Interviewer: What is your working schedule?

Taylor: When I'm teaching I don't work much on my manuscripts. I keep them open on my desk, look at them every morning, but I don't press myself. But that's just September to Christmas. After Christmas it's different. I devote myself entirely to my writing. I tell myself that my mornings are my writing time, no matter where I am. After an early breakfast I go to my study. Now I may not really write—do you?—often my mind wanders off, I do other things, or I think of some other manuscript. It may be eleven before I really get going. I'll be there daydreaming, and then suddenly the thing just starts coming. And then I go on until I eat lunch at two or something. But I have got to the point now where I can write pretty well anywhere at any time. Writing is almost like ladies' knitting, I always have it with me.

Interviewer: That wasn't always true?

Taylor: No indeed. For a long time I couldn't write except under the strictest conditions—just the way I'd written before. I began writing on the arm of a swing, on the back porch of our house—those first stories that Allen Tate liked. And for a long time I couldn't write anywhere else. Just superstition. I *had* to write on the swing on the back porch.

Interviewer: The uncertainty of a beginning writer.

Taylor: Yes. You know you have to have two things when you begin to write. You have to have some instinct for writing stories— you may write your first stories just from that, entirely—but you also have to have some ability to learn how you did it and how it's done: how to improve upon it.

I so often see young writers who do what I did, which is to write two or three stories that were quite good, and then for several years not be able to write a decent story because I was so self-conscious about it, afraid that I'd make some awful mistake with what I was doing and discovering and learning. That's when I think it is helpful to have an older writer to talk to about your work—who can say what's good about it. Often you know it's good, but you don't know how you did it.

But I still like to write on a porch swing! In Key West I have a swing on the porch that I like to sit in to write. It gives you something to do, keeps you from smoking—you push yourself, your feet go. . .

Interviewer: The fallow time, just pushing the swing, is very important, then?

Taylor: Your images depend on parts of you that you don't control. You can't just "work up" an image. You find the right way of telling the story through your dreams or something—it's very much more like that.

Interviewer: Do you ever do research for a story?

Taylor: No, I feel very strongly against that. I read Southern history because I *like* reading it, and then suddenly I'll find it appearing in something I write. But as soon as I have a body of ideas and put them in a story consciously, that just kills it for me. When I have done it at times, it *has* killed it. I have a number of stories I've never put in a collection and never would put in a collection, partly because it seemed to me they never came to life on their own. I had forced some idea, something Freudian or political or some idea about history.

Interviewer: I was trying to write something last week and found I couldn't go on until I found a street map of the city it took place in—

Taylor: Well, I might do that. If I didn't remember something, I might look it up, or correct it afterward, but usually my tendency is just to go on. I've had things terribly wrong, and had editors straighten me out, *The New Yorker* particularly. In "The Old Forest" *The New Yorker* called and said our historian tells us such-and-such, for instance that the trees had not been there as long as I said they had been there (the trees in that forest) or the city was not founded by the person I said it was founded by. I said Andrew Jackson laid out the city, and they said it was General Winchester. Well, General Winchester and General Jackson were in business together; they were land speculators. So I had it wrong, but I didn't care.

Interviewer: You left it?

Taylor: I think I changed it. It didn't matter. But there were some things I left, that they corrected me on. I said, well, for the sake of the story what's important is the legend I grew up with.

I've always had a dislike of any form of didacticism, especially when it becomes the dominant element in writing. Character and emotional content should always be the strong elements. I think that was maybe what went wrong with my early novel, that I wanted it to be too profound, and I was trying to put too much into it. I learned fairly early that you can handle so little *idea* in a story. Well, *I* can!

Interviewer: But memory is very important, isn't it? What is your earliest memory?

Taylor: Standing on the lawn of the house at Trenton and seeing a wild sunset, reds, a red-brick sunset, a thing which both exhilarated and terrified me, being out there alone. And another early memory— I was alone again, I played alone a lot, although I had brothers and

sisters around—was of seeing the first airplane that I'd ever seen. A
little one. They never landed near Trenton. Seeing that tiny plane up
in the sky, knowing a man was in it, made me feel very lonely.

Interviewer: Do you think a great memory is important for a
writer?

Taylor: You have to have a great memory for trivia, for details that
are specific and that you want to remember. I do have a good
memory. A while ago I got a letter from John Berryman's first wife,
Eileen Simpson, a brilliant woman. She sent me a part of a chapter of
a book she was writing about Lowell and Berryman and all that. Until
I read it, I hadn't known that I remembered every detail from the first
crack-up Lowell ever had. Well of course it was very important: he
was visiting us, there was no hospital that would accept him and we
had to put him in jail, and his mother and Dr. Merrill Moore flew in
and took him back to Boston.

It was a long story, part of it heartbreaking and part of it very
funny. Allen Tate had called me from Chicago and said, "Cal is not
himself at all," and that he and Caroline had just put him on a train!
Well, of course I was furious—Allen had no business putting him on a
train. But I also knew that Allen had a great dramatic sense, and I
thought he must be exaggerating. I didn't think it was true when he
said that Cal was beside himself, that—I don't think *this was* true—
that he tried to molest a child at the railroad station. Anyhow, he'd
behaved strangely, frightened a child on the platform, and picked up
Allen and carried him down the platform. Allen was very small.
Anyhow, Allen said I was to meet him with the police at the railroad
station!

Well that was *something*! because some time before that, when the
Tates were in Maine visiting the Lowells, Caroline had thrown a
peanut butter jar at Jean [Stafford Lowell] and Jean ran and called
the sheriff, saying, "I feared for my life." And Allen was outraged and
said, "You don't call the police on your friends."

Interviewer: Why did she do it? Throw the peanut-butter jar?

Taylor: Oh, Jean said Allen was having an affair with a certain
young literary woman, and that infuriated Caroline. She started
throwing things at Jean. . . .

But anyway, as soon as Cal stepped off the train I could see he was
out of his head. He wasn't the Lowell I knew. He was dirty and

dishevelled. So I took him to the faculty club and put him up there instead of taking him home. We had a new baby, and I told him the baby was not well. But while we were having dinner in this place, he began to sniff and say, "Do you smell that?" I said no, and he said, "I know what it is, it's brimstone. He's over there behind the fern." I took him to his room, and went to my house, but a few minutes later I was called by the people at the club. They said he had come out of his room and run through the kitchen terrorizing the cooks, and then run out into the streets,

I spent the early part of the night searching for him, going through the streets calling "Lowell, Lowell" at the top of my voice. In the meantime he'd gone up to a movie house and stolen a roll of tickets, just reached in and grabbed the tickets and run off down the street! By now the police were looking for him too. We were all running around the town—Bloomington is not a big town!—and finally he knocked on a door that happened to be a policeman's house, and they took him in.

For me the most traumatic part of it was the next morning. I was just beside myself because we had been the closest friends—room-mates and all—and I thought it was the end. I never thought he would be sane again. So the next morning I went down there to the jail, and he was in a block of cells, and there was nobody there with him. They let me in and locked the gate, and I went into the cell with him. I was scared to death. Finally I said, "Cal, let's pray," and he said, "Let's get down here and pray together to get out of this place." And I said—because I was scared—"Cal, I never could pray in the same room with anybody." So I went into the next cell, and we got down on our knees and prayed in adjoining cells. But then time went by, and they changed guards. The new guard hadn't been told I wasn't also an inmate! I was in there four hours with him. I would call for them to let me out, and Cal would say "That's not Christian. You call for them to let me out and I'll call for them to let you out!"

Interviewer: I know you haven't written memoirs, but do you write critical essays or reviews?

Taylor: The last review I wrote was a review of Allen Tate's *The Fathers,* which came out, I think, in 1939.

I resolved early that if I was going to teach, I was never going to write criticism, and I won't. It's too hard. Why, writing criticism takes

as much time as writing fiction and is a much less serious business!
Teaching takes as much of my life as I want to give to generalization.
And I like teaching so much better than I like writing criticism. It
involves you with other people. I do all my teaching in conference,
one to one, Teaching is always done best vis-a-vis. I worked in New
York for a time at Henry Holt, just as a first reader, and I realized I
disliked reading all those manuscripts from people I would never see
or know anything about. It is so much more fun to see really bright
young people trying to write and learning to read intelligently, and
seeing them develop, being involved with them. So much of your life
as a writer is isolating. When I think of that, I can hardly wait for my
next teaching stint at some college or university.

   And then, too, I have a horror of defining, of limiting. Everything
seems to me to be such a cliché as soon as I say it. And the other
thing is, as soon as I make a point, I am sure I can disprove it, am
sure that the opposite is also true!

Interviewer: You once said something in that context about
Flaubert—

Taylor: Yes, well, of course who can write fiction in this century
without feeling some pressure from Flaubert? And some of the writers
I've been influenced by, to them Flaubert was God. His was the
Word. He was the Master. But you know, often I think of Flaubert's
rules and regulations and wish to see if I can successfully defy them.
To see how much the narrator can generalize and how much he can
come in and exercise his omniscience, how far I can impose the
narrator on the narrative. Because, you know, I believe if one thing
can be proved by some aesthetic theory, then there is inevitably
another theory that can prove the opposite true. . . . And the
delightful thing about writing stories is that when you actually write a
story, you can have it both ways. You can mull it over and cover up
and deceive the reader until finally he accepts your way of doing it.
The best thing of all is that you don't have to be consistent,
particularly from one story to another. When I was still an undergraduate I wrote a story called "The Spinster's Tale," and the next
story after that was called "The Fancy Woman," in which I absolutely
reversed the characters and the subject. What I wished to present in
that first story was a discovery of evil, how the shock of it affected a
woman's whole life. And in the other story the character was so far

corrupted that she couldn't believe in her discovery of innocence. She was beyond any possibility of accepting it. Maybe that is not the right way to write, but I often bounce from one idea to another. So often ideas for stories are born out of other stories. You write one, and in it you see some little minor theme in there that you wish to develop further.

Interviewer: When I was reading your stories chronologically in one fell swoop, I was conscious that many of them seemed concerned with revising some view of the past, or with present events in which the past is a vital element.

Taylor: I think that's one way of thinking about one's fiction. Saying, well, what if I looked at it from this other point of view? Taking stories one has heard and trying to make sense of them, trying to learn what in the closest analysis and profoundest speculation they might mean.

In the beginning I wrote many stories about women. Southern women, old ladies, a lot of them. Each story came out of some incident, out of some strong feeling. I am always trying to discover in a story what it is that I am *really* trying to say about the subject and why it interests me, what it means and what I can do with it. In "Miss Leonora When Last Seen", for instance, I was trying to imagine what it was like to have *been* one of those women I was writing about. To reflect *that* side, that world.

Interviewer: Miss Leonora as the representative of her sex and class and world.

Taylor: After that I decided I had written all I had to say about old ladies! Not that it was such a wonderful story, but I felt I had got much more to the point in that story of what an old lady in the South represented as a sort of ideal character. I had been working toward that always, but never going quite as directly at it as that—

Interviewer: Her fidelity to a certain code of behavior?

Taylor: What was asked of her. That certain things were asked of her, and she went on answering. Her representing certain ideals that were no longer held by the rising generation. And then trying to characterize such a woman, aside from the ideals. To discover what a story means and how to push it, and yet to keep it naturalistic and a mere story.

I had seen such women, and I wanted to discover what they

meant, what their lives meant. The women that I had seen were the most cultivated people I knew, so much more cultivated than the men in that society. And they had ideas—not explicit ideas, but inceptions of ideas as to what the world should be like, what their roles were to be. I had grown up with just so many old ladies: my father, being a lawyer, looked after the estates and affairs of many old ladies; wherever we were living they'd come to visit us, with their wardrobe trunks. They were delightful, extremely intelligent people. They stood for the intellectual and cultural life of the society.

Interviewer: Jane Barnes suggests in her essay about you that after "Miss Leonora. . ." you began to explore the masculine side of life, of your own nature.

Taylor: I think she hits the nail on the head. In the beginning my sympathy had been all with women, but after that I thought, well, what if I look at it from the men's point of view of that world. . . . My wife says I'm much softer, easier on my father now when I tell stories. That his role changes in them from the way I used to tell them. When I was first married, my father and I had battles. My mother and father would come to visit, and my father would insist on staying in bed and having his breakfast brought to him. And I would rage and say, "He can't *do* that!" and Eleanor would say, "Oh yes." She would take his meals up, or my mother would. She remembers my raging—but I had other feelings about him, also.

Interviewer: I remember an early story, "Porte Cochere," in which the father seems very like the man in "The Gift of the Prodigal" but less sympathetically viewed.

Taylor: The man in the later stories is much more sympathetic than that man in the earlier. I like that story dramatically—that's what I was trying to do then, learn to write a dramatic story—but I feel I never got inside that man in "Porte Cochere." I had someone tell me just this week that it's mechanically fine, dramatically witty, the language is satisfactory, but something is missing, something about getting inside the character. I don't think you engage in that story emotionally.

I think the new stories have that. I like to think I have made some progress. One makes advances. You *do!* You come to see what your story is like and what you want to get in it. That's part of the fun: to see how you can get the other elements that are not your natural interests or concerns primarily. In that earlier story I was trying to force it really dramatically. He was not a character of the sort I was interested in at that time. I could probably write that story better now because I have more interest in that sort of person, maybe because since then I have seen my father and others grow old. And grown old myself. I can be more sympathetic.

Interviewer: After "Miss Leonora" the next story was—

Taylor: "Venus, Cupid, Folly and Time." I had got to the point where I had become interested in making up stories. Ford Madox Ford says at some point you have to begin to make up stories. Up until then in some stories—the most anthologized like "What You Hear from 'Em?"—there's not a word that's made up.

But "Venus, Cupid, Folly and Time" begins a change in my writing. It is less ironic, less funny, with fewer genteel characters, more eccentrics. I still like it as a story, but when it came out, Randall Jarrell didn't like it. He told me so.

Interviewer: Was that important to you?

Taylor: We were very close at that time. In fact we bought a "duplex" together. It was great fun. He'd go over my stories and over Eleanor's poems. He loved to do that, and he'd say devastating things sometimes, but good things. I think he was the finest critic of the generation; it is a delight to read him. He would spend just an amazing amount of time on his friends' work, would settle down for a whole afternoon over a story or a poem. But you know I don't think it was altogether good. In the end you have to throw over your mentor. In my stories he didn't like it whenever I introduced anything very severe. He wanted me to have a very light touch, Chekhovian, not to have much serious event in it. I think he really thought of me as the Southern regional writer of memoir stories. He used to say, "Write all those stories you can, because that is a world that's gone, will never exist again, and this record of it should exist." So when that story, "Venus, Cupid, Folly and Time" came out, he was very unsympathetic. Your friends often do this, when you want to change and are trying to do something else, and they've liked that other you. But you know, I never could go back and write those stories, the tone of which pretended to be just memoirs of genteel families.

Interviewer: I remember your saying that "Venus, Cupid . . ." was your first plotted story—"made" rather than evolved. You started with an effect to be achieved rather than a tale to be told?

Taylor: I really had in mind almost an allegory. One of the things that it was is a story about incest—not just the brother and sister, but all the young people. It's a form of incest to want to marry only in your own class, your own background exactly. That was the world I had grown up in. I had seen my brother and sisters in it. And some of those young people—it was very sad—*couldn't* marry anyone but that way, and never married because there was nobody in that set for them. They had other chances to marry, but nobody that would fit; it had to be "in the family," so to speak. It *is* a sort of incest to marry within a class, especially when it's within a class in a certain town. People didn't like it as well if they married somebody from Cincinnati or New Orleans; it had to be somebody from Memphis or Nashville. That was what my idea was. I had a much clearer synopsis for that story in my mind than I usually do. That really was a turning point.

Interviewer: You often start with just an image, or a single sentence, don't you? In "The Fancy Woman" it was that first sentence?

Taylor: Yes. I feel justified in doing that because if you have any profound thoughts or profound views, they will emerge from within the story inevitably. I still believe that. I tell young writers not to worry about writing a profound story because, as James said, a profound mind will produce a profound story and a superficial mind will produce a superficial story. Remember Tolstoy's saying of Chekhov that Chekhov was so given to truth that he could not possibly have presented anything but the truth. And he said—Tolstoy said that it's very much the way it was when he was learning to ride a bicycle. He was learning in a huge gymnasium, and there was one lady, standing in the middle, and he kept saying to himself, 'Whatever I do I must not run into that woman! And he circled around her—he could hardly ride the bicycle—and ran her down. That's the way Chekhov is with the truth, Tolstoy said. Whatever he *tries* to do. . . .

Interviewer: And telling the truth is, finally, what writing is about? That wonderful quote from Montaigne about speaking the truth, not as much as you know but as much as you dare—and daring more as you grow older.

Taylor: I think trying to write is a religious exercise. You are trying to understand life, and you can only get the illusion of doing it fully by writing. That is, it's the only way I can come to understand things fully. When I create, when I put my own mark on something and form it, I begin to know the whole truth about it, how it was put together. Then you can begin to change things around. You know all this after you have written a lot. You really know. And it has become the most important thing in your life. It has nothing to do with craft, or even art, in a way. It is making sense of life. It is coming to understand yourself.

That's what I love about Katherine Anne Porter—the natural writer that she is. She managed to interpret the events of her life in her stories, just by writing them down. She knew what she was really like—that represents the highest intelligence in the world, to know what you really are. She did. You think of a storyteller as not very intellectual at all—or I do—someone who writes stories lets his intelligence come out *that* way. But she was intellectual in the ordinary sense, too. Her essays are just amazing. And you know, though she knew her art—there was no question about that—she was my idea of the unprofessional.

I feel so strongly against professionalism, against someone's feeling he has to write a book every year to keep his name before the public. I see people pressing themselves, torturing themselves, for that, rather than writing out of a compulsion some story from their own experience, their own feelings. That's the way you should write, unless you are just practicing. I tell young writers to steal a plot or an idea or whatever, just to get going. See how a character comes out, how you fit it into your life. . . . You see great writers doing it too. Certainly some of James' stories came right out of Trollope. And some came from Hawthorne. It's just so clear to me that James took the work of Hawthrone and Trollope and of all kinds of writers and made out of them a much greater work. I think he is much greater than any of the others.

I really don't think you should make money writing. Oh, I'm not going to turn down money, but people worrying about how they are going to make a living writing ought to worry about making a living some other way on the periphery, doing something congenial to them like teaching or editing. We hear a lot of complaints from writers now, especially from PEN, about the situation of the writer—well, it's *always* been awful! I think you should write for yourself, for the joy of it, the pleasure of it, and for the satisfaction that you have in learning about your life.

Interviewer: What about hack work, copywriting or journalism or—

Taylor: Some good novelists have done it. It depends on the energy of the person, whether you can afford to waste that much. If you have enough money, I don't think you should do anything but write, but if you have to earn a living, there is nothing pleasanter than teaching!

Interviewer: What about the alleged insularity of academic life, the Ivory Tower?

Taylor: The people who are affected by that insularity would be affected by something else. I certainly don't think it hurt Warren and all that generation who taught. Some people can live in an academic community and yet write about other things—if you've had a fairly rich life, and especially if you live in the part of the world where you've always lived, and know people. I've always made a point wherever we've lived, teaching, of having most of my friends from the town, non-academic people. In Charlottesville our best friends are not the academics. I want to be part of a community. When I taught at Ohio State—I did it for 6 years—we found a house at the farthest end of Columbus, in a completely unacademic community. Not because we didn't like the others, but so as not to live entirely inside it, just for my own satisfaction. But if you're a writer, if you have something to say, you can find it in anything—you can write about academics. They're people too!

Interviewer: In the last years you've been writing stories in a new form. Prose poems? What do you call them?

Taylor: Lowell always spoke of them as "story poems" in his homey way. That's better. I have learned not to speak of them as poems, myself. I call them broken-line prose. I began writing them when I was trying to make things shorter. I am always trying for compression. It fascinates me that my stories get longer and longer when I'm always trying to make them shorter and shorter. I don't think there are many very great *short* stories in the language— Kipling's "Lispeth" and Katherine Anne's "Magic."

I began by wanting to get interest in every line, every sentence. I felt if a line is broken, if where the line ends means something, you get another emphasis. When a sentence just ends at that line, you get one line of rhythm, one emphasis, but if it ends in the middle of the line, you get something else, the run-on lines, enjambment. All these are techniques of poetry. Oh, the sentences mean what they mean, but the fact that they're put together in a line gives another emphasis, the way it does in poetry. You have the two kinds of syntax, the line-endings and the run-on line, and the regular syntax of the language. You can be saying a lot more in a short space.

This was my feeling when I began writing them, not really *knowing* what I was doing. For years I was very sanctimonious, saying, "I like poetry to be poetry and fiction to be fiction." In my case that's a sure sign that someday I'm going to change my mind and do just the opposite. I began by writing just a few lines that way, in the story called "Three Heroines." It was easy to write because it's almost literally what happened: an account of my going home, and my mother and the woman that had always looked after her. The story just fell into place, and I was able to work on the lines, working out the form.

Every story in *In the Miro District* was written in that form originally. That is, I began them all that way, but if I got halfway through and found that they got too long, or I couldn't sustain it, or that the line ends were not significant, no longer functional, then I gave it up. But most of the time I think it puts more emphasis on the texture of the thing if you think of it in terms of lines, if you think of the intrinsic interest of each sentence. That is my ideal in writing, that each sentence should have an intrinsic interest, and then that it should have an interest in terms of the whole story. That is the satisfaction that you get in poetry, and this is the way I think of writing a story. Even the novel-like thing I'm writing now is being written in that form.

Interviewer: Have you ever written a "real" novel?

Taylor: One that I never published, and finally destroyed. It was the only really long full-length novel I ever wrote. It was about a young man in a city like Memphis, an artist, a painter, a writer, who goes away to New York. It's about his love affair with an older woman. Then years later he comes back. It's about his growing up and his discovery of the world outside, and his failures as an artist, really. But it never satisfied me—his relation to his background, and then his discovery of what he was to do with his life and how it related to the world he'd come out of. This just never worked. The poetry of it didn't work, the poetry of character and context, which is what I care most about. You never know why something fails exactly, except I think I had too many diverse themes going at one time. I thought that was what one did in a novel, but for me it didn't work.

I think what really failed in that novel was the theme of cultural environment, growing up as a Southerner in a Southern city and *not* rejecting it. Most artists that come from the provinces in this country finally just reject it completely. And this was an effort to deal with his not rejecting it, his being influenced always by these experiences of his growing up and trying to discover what life is all about.

Finally, just to get it out of my system, I managed to make a sort of synopsis of it in a play called "The Early Guest." The Drama Department at Charlottesville did two performances of it, with masks and all sorts of things. There is absolutely not a laugh in the whole play, it's dead serious, without any irony, and one performance was done for a big audience, and I thought it was an excellent flop. But then it was presented again to a small high-brow audience of people just wild about the theater, and I thought it was a great success—and that was some consolation.

Interviewer: Once to Stephen Goodwin you spoke of the short story as a dramatic form, more akin to playwriting than to the writing of novels—

Taylor: The short story writer is concerned with compression, with saying as much as he can in a short space, just as the poet is. So he has to choose the right dramatic moment for the presentation, and he becomes concerned with that, with finding the right moment to tell the story. If you do that in writing a story, you can have as big a canvas as you do in a novel. You can, if you've found exactly the right moment for vital interplay between the characters and for presenting the events and the context of the story. That's the genius of the short story writer—finding precisely those moments.

I think the same is true for playwrights. In a play everything has to be done in a particular scene, at a particular time, and you have to choose that. That's the business of the dramatist.

Interviewer: Choosing what the curtain rises on, say, in *The Cherry Orchard?*

Taylor: Yes, the curtain goes up and the trees are being cut. You'll find that Chekhov and Pirandello and all the great short story writers—well, so many of the great short story writers—ended by writing plays that were their major works. Chekhov, the Irish playwrights. And the only really boring thing Chekhov ever wrote was his one effort at novel writing, *The Shooting Party.*

But in this country there's always been pressure on short story writers to become novelists. It's easier to sell a novel than to sell a short story, really, and so there's economic pressure to write novels. So many short story writers that I know have agonized for years trying to write the novel that was going to make them rich or famous. And often it does. It's strange: Katherine Anne Porter is famous because of *Ship of Fools,* which is not nearly as good as her stories, and Robert Penn Warren is famous for his novels, which are not nearly as good as his poems. And I think that Faulkner is a greater short story writer than novelist.

Interviewer: Did you know him?

Taylor: No, I never knew him either in Nashville or in Memphis, but when I was overseas, in my early twenties, my sister would see Faulkner at parties. She was a very attractive person, and she would tell him that she had a younger brother who intended to be a writer, and he would give her advice which she wrote to me. I have somewhere her letters telling me what to read, what to do. And one of the things he said was to "Read *Anna Karenina* and *Anna Karenina* and *Anna Karenina,*" which was marvelous advice, I think, but I wouldn't have supposed he would have said just that about that book.

This went on during the war, while I was overseas, and then I met him afterwards, and he would have nothing to do with me! Oh, he would acknowledge my existence and so on, but he really didn't like other writers. The only writer I ever knew whom he liked was Shelby Foote. He's a wonderful historian. I admire especially his Civil War histories. He and Faulkner became good friends. I can see that they temperamentally would have had something in common other than their literary interests—masculine interests in hunting and such things.

Interviewer: You spoke earlier of trying to shorten and compress, but I have the impression that your most recent stories are often very long.

Taylor: I'm not trying now to write short stories. A really short story has to be concerned with a limited kind of experience, and be limited in time, I think. But if your tendency is to write longer and longer stories, then you should go ahead, I think.

For one thing, I've got terribly interested in plot, a thing I scorned when I was a young man. When people would mention plot to me, or structure even, I was repelled. I thought there was something crass about plot. I had no interest in it. But I've learned though the years that there's something very useful in it, that there is a kind of emphasis you can achieve with plot used properly. It *punctuates!* It can say, "Well, we've gone this far" and then "this far."

Interviewer: I know you admire Mann. Was this interest in plot and structure something you saw in him?

Taylor: I'm very admiring of the structure of Mann's stories— "Tonio Kroger" and "Disorder and Early Sorrow" and "Death in Venice." I had always admired Tolstoy's stories, but when I came to Mann's—well, I'd always thought I knew what a short story was and what a novel was, but when I read those stories, I saw that here was something that seemed to be able to do the best of both.

James loved that form too, that of the long story, but his are a different sort of thing altogether. Lowell used to make fun and say I was the master of the long short novel or the short long story, something like that—but I think there *is* a difference. In Mann or some of Turgenev's stories that I admire, like "Old Portraits," a whole life is suggested, which is not what James' short novels do. Those are much more tightly made and focus on one certain area of experience. Jarrell didn't like James' stories because he said, "You see how mechanically made they are!" Well I like them, but they don't—well some of them *do* suggest a whole world, some suggest the same world that he gets in his great novels—but in these stories of Mann's you have it every way. As the story moves, the character is revealed, the whole world opens up. That's what's very impressive to me. I don't feel that one could see any influence in my stories. It was many years before I could even attempt such a thing, but the conception was very influential for a very long time. . . . Do you know "Disorder and Early Sorrow"?

Interviewer: Yes.

Taylor: What I do so admire about it is the whole period in history that seems to come out of that story. He has the historian, and then the drama between the young people in the story—so that it is very significant *where* and *when* it takes place, the poetry of character and context. And very dramatic. But without the need to reveal every part of a life.

Interviewer: As you would feel in a novel?

Taylor: Well, in a long story you still do what you do in a short story, but at the same time you suggest a great deal about the world; you imply and suggest more. In a novel you expect more explication. A story like Katherine Anne Porter's "Old Mortality" suggests whole worlds. Almost every page suggests much more than is there— history, psychology, everything.

Interviewer: But, it's still something that can be read in one sitting.

Taylor: That's what I like to think of. These long stories that I'm writing are something that can be read in one evening. That's what I love, to settle in for a long evening's reading, several hours.

I think there's no reason to define what's a novel and what's a story finally, but in a novel you can often say—with Dreiser or someone— that it's the cumulative effect that counts. It can be very dull and bad in parts. There's not a page in Thomas Wolfe that I would really say I admire, and yet in the end he does have an impact. I think that's true to a lesser degree of many other important novelists, that they're not concerned with making every sentence do the kind of work that a short story writer must. In fact, if you try to write a novel the way you write a poem or a short story, you end up with *Finnegans Wake,* and I think that's a dead end. It shows genius. Only a genius could have written it, but does anybody read it except the scholars?

And you can't sustain it—or *I* can't. I find that in trying to write my poem-like stories, that when I write the first ten pages, I think they're going to be short and I'm packing everything in. I began both "The Captain's Son" and "In the Miro District" in that form. But when I realized halfway through that both of those stories were going to be complicated and long, I lost the lines. They were no longer signifi- cant, the line ends. And when the line ends are no longer significant, then you know it's just an artificial thing. But I went on and wrote them that way anyhow. And "The Gift of the Prodigal" I submitted to *The New Yorker* in that form. I knew all along they wouldn't like it that way. I didn't like it either—I did it sort of for fun. And they wrote back at once, saying they'd like to print it, but they'd like me to put it in the other form. And I said I would, but that I'd like the right, if I put it in a book, to put it back in the other form. I haven't done so, however.

I still find that the most satisfying way to begin, feeling that every sentence, every phrase must have some intrinsic interest as well as relate to the larger interest of the story. To me that's what's fun about writing. It's like saying that life makes sense! Pretending that the small diurnal things make sense! Which of course they don't.

Interviewer: We haven't talked about what makes Southern fiction unique—why there have been so many first-rate fiction writers in the last century. What was the impact of the War, of being the first Americans to be invaded, to experience defeat?

Taylor: I think that was very strong in it. But there are other things that were important as far as Southern fiction is concerned. I think the whole country, the whole Western world, was turning from an agrarian society into an industrial urban society, and in the South, because of the War, it was a dramatic change, a dramatic coincidence—

It's the same thing that you see in Chekhov. The characters in Chekhov's plays are people who are ineffectual, living in circumstances in which the family doesn't work, the farm doesn't work, the whole society doesn't work. The characters that Chekhov chose to write about are more dramatic because they coincide with the moment of change in the whole society.

And this is what happened in the South, I think. Faulkner and the other writers, the Agrarians generally, defined this. They could see it. They didn't speak for the world—in fact the Nashville Agrarians were saying it was a Southern phenomenon—but the fact is, it was going on all over the world. Chesterton and the Decentralists in England had already been writing. There was resistance to this change, to the modernization of society which foresaw the end of the family when the family was no longer a viable economic unit, when the farm economy was no longer the principal economy. The rest of the world had families too, but the South saw the family changing and focused on that. The family was very important politically here. Not just to Faulkner, but to Caroline Gordon and all the serious fiction writers of the period. That's *why* the rest of the world found it fascinating, even though the world might not have known why it was fascinated. I don't think critics took the line that "this is what's happening to the world," but it was so. And I think that's the way writers find their best subjects. I don't mean they set about to do it, but when a writer becomes as good as Faulkner, it's because there has been a wonderful amazing coincidence between his themes and the circumstances of his day.

Interviewer: What about young Southern writers? Is the South still distinct as a culture?

Taylor: There are a lot of young writers from the rural South or from the small towns of the South who are still very much interested in what's happened there. Writing fiction is discovery. Faulkner and the other writers of his generation and the prior generation too were discovering what it was like to be a Southerner, what it was like to be an American and at the same time a Southerner. This mixed loyalty to country and to region is disturbingly strong and will continue to disturb Southerners.

It's the Southern cities that I have always been so much interested in, and the Southern country people who moved to the cities after the Civil War, carrying with them the mores and the general customs of the country, the general belief that the country was good and the city was bad. I think this prevailed all through my childhood and growing up, and until the Second World War. But the cities now— Atlanta, Nashville, Memphis, New Orleans—have been invaded by the rest of the country; these cities have been changed. I don't have any statistics, but I would imagine that of the population of Memphis, say, there'd be a large portion who have been there for only one generation, who came from various parts of the country, and are not Southern. And there has ceased to be, almost, that feeling of being different from the national population.

You know, in *The Mind of the South,* Cash says that the South really began at Appomattox, that "The South" didn't exist before the Civil War. I don't know whether he's the first that said that, but he points out that the same families held power in the South after the Civil War as before. The notion had developed, I think, until he wrote that book, that a whole new class of people had come in and got rich. I think Cash was right. I used not to, but I do now. A lot of people stayed in the country, as you see in the Faulkner novels, but a lot of the same families moved to the city and were the powerful people there, and dominate still the society of those towns in every sense of the word. And they invented the idea of a golden age, of the older order. . . .

One of the things Cash points out is the insistence upon kinship. You know, the old jokes about cousin so-and-so, all that. They did that in order to re-establish the power of the same class of people who had been in power before; they had to stand together against the Blacks and against the carpetbaggers. Thus to acknowledge any possible kin, even with what they called the plain people, with all the people that were of lower economic class—that bound them together. My own grandfather, who was in politics, did that. He claimed kin with everyone—at least with all the people of the same name as his, who before the War he wouldn't have acknowledged as kin at all.

Interviewer: Hasn't there been a real change in the world of your stories over the years? I have the sense that in the early work the characters go back to actual places and relationships to replenish their sense of self—but that lately, starting perhaps with A *Stand in the Mountains* what nourishes them seems to be an invented or crystallized past held in their own minds.

Taylor: I think that is true. It's a different world from the world I began writing about where families did exist as little groups, and if they went out of the South, they took the South with them. It's true to a far lesser degree now. The concern now is for what sort of adjustments we are making to this, how we shall live without it.

Interviewer: Without that old sense of belonging, of connectedness, even when it was bitter, abrasive?

Taylor: I think that sense is part of what people mean when they talk about what the Southern temper is, and what is isn't, and how it is to be distinguished. A lot of it is the strong family tradition, I'm sure. A sense of community, of knowing who they are. And then the feeling that in a national sense they *don't* know who they are. The Southern writer has been trying to assert, to discover, that identity. And that's when it's wonderful, when writers are discovering things. This has happened in other times. The English were doing it in the 19th century in their fiction: Trollope defined English country life, village life and the life of the highest echelons too. All the 19th century English writers were doing it. And to a lesser degree that is what Southern writers have been doing in this century. We are—the South is—a much smaller country than England, of course. In a sense you could do a map of the South in which you put Memphis 50 miles from Charleston, because that is the reality. There are these vast spaces in between that are just wasteland.

Interviewer: We've talked a great deal about family but nothing much about marriage. How has it been, having two writers in the household?

Taylor: Eleanor has simply made it possible. Another thing was that we married fairly young, and both families were living. Neither of us was alienated from parents or from his culture. And we came along in that Southern agrarian movement and were terribly interested in it, both of us.

But the main thing was Eleanor. When our children came along, she just made up her mind not to think of her writing much. I mean she wouldn't admit she was writing—if you write, you write! She devoted herself to the children and to being the daughter-in-law and the sister-in-law. She said she wasn't going to have a competition between the children and the work. It was a risk because she might not have lived, something might have happened at any rate—but she did, she survived, and then she began writing again.

And I always kept a job. The main reason I've always taught is that I didn't want to pit my family against my writing either.

But you know, after the children were gone, after we had played the traditional roles completely, we were in complete agreement that now we each were going to pursue our own selves, express our own tastes, live as we want to, exactly, for some part of the year, and to write independently. In some ways we both write better in separate houses in different parts of the world! But the marriage was so cemented that it works for us. Eleanor and I totally disagree on so many things, and yet we are able to because we have all this past in common, the family thing, and our affection for each other, and the children. But we totally disagree on all sorts of major topics of the day. She's all for abortion, so I find myself taking more and more the other line. . . .

I can't stop on this subject, but I can't go on, on the other hand, because it's such a mystery why people *do* get along. But then we did, all those years. . . . Jarrell used to say, I flatter myself, that we were the two best writers that have been married to each other. He adored Eleanor.

And then, I guess you have to talk in terms of psychology some. We had other role models. Even though when we lived in Memphis or Nashville or Norwood all our friends were divorcing like fury and marrying again, we had others like John Crowe Ransom and his wife who were married for fifty years or more. They were very attractive, bright people, and we were very close to them. Many of those people in the South, the Agrarians, even Allen Tate—who married a number of times—was married a long time first to Caroline Gordon. When we married, Caroline was there at the wedding as the mother of the bride so to speak, and they became our parents in a way. We were close to them always. We did not reject our traditional values and our backgrounds. I think Southerners are less likely to, than are people from other parts of the country.

And then as other people want other things, I wanted *family*. I wanted to go on into this world seeing myself as living in a family. In a way it was a great *interest* of mine, an intellectual interest, I consider it—keeping in touch, remaining in the family, the larger family, as we have. From a very early age my mother taught me that you should never say "in-law," "brother-in-law"; it was always "my brother." That expresses something of the insistence upon the power of the family.

I purposely kept going back. A lot of the members of my family cut themselves off. . . . And now of course there's the question of whether the family is going to continue as the basic cultural and economic unit of our society. It can't be, in a society which is based on large industrial development, in which it is the individual's relationship to the state or the big industry that matters, not to the family. But I think it is a barbarous country in which the family is not the basic unit because that means an end to the relationships between people of various age groups and—inevitably, in the extended family—various economic groups. We always had poor relations and rich relations and common relations. You might not admit it, but you had distant cousins you didn't like. During the 60s and 70s when my children and other children were living in communes, I would say that's not nearly as good a commune as the family commune, because it's easy to love people who are your age and exactly your position in life, but it's not so easy to love babies and trembling old people.

And this is what happened in our society in the last generation. It began when they began the consolidation of schools. I wrote "Miss Leonora When Last Seen" in simple protest. You sent your children off to those vast public schools, miles away, and the children saw their peers all day long. This was their real life. And then they were bused back to this other community, their families, that were different. And they came back with a certain contempt for their family, for their customs and manners. It meant finally the state taking over bringing up children, but not taking on the real responsibility.

I know I sound like an old crank, but I think there really is a great sickness in the country—families are broken and people have no relations except with their own generation. They have better race relations with other people in their generation, but they don't have any relation with the very old and the very young, with people who are eccentrics, who are totally different from them.

We all know how difficult it was to live in families, what a nightmare families are, what a nightmare marriage is. The family's the worst institution ever invented—but only if society is not supportive. If all society is not built upon it, there's no power in it. Power is very important. If there is no power in the family, then it's just a constraint and a burden. I know better than anybody, as a Southerner and as a member of large families, how terribly you paid, but then see what you pay by this isolation, and the kind of dependency that you get from old people's homes, the indifference of bureaucrats. The humanity of the family is lost and lost forever. The particularity of life is lost when we are just so many isolated creatures.

I don't know any solution for it, because for me it all hinges on that tiny little thing, the consolidation of schools. And the breakdown of the small community within this enormous community, all over the country.

Interviewer: How would you like to be remembered?

Taylor: I would like to have as many of my stories as possible survive and be read and liked. At my age it's hard not to want to feel that your last book is your best book. And I'd like to feel that what I'm doing now is still better. When I look back on my earlier things, I understand why a lot of them were ignored. They're not bad, they're not slick or cheap in any way, but I lacked knowledge of how to say what I wanted to say, and lacked knowledge of what I wanted to say.

I always had the inclination to tell a story, but in my early stories I never pressed hard enough to know what it meant, as I think I do now. I wasted many years of effort writing things that were not the kinds of stories I should have been writing. I'm not ashamed of any of them, but I wish I'd written other stories that I would like to write now.

Interviewer: What are you working on now?

Taylor: I consider it bad luck to talk about what you're going to write—bad luck and boring to the listener. I have completed the second draft of a novel—or a long, long story—two hundred fifty pages. And I have put it away for a time. And I have about a hundred pages on another. Both have the same setting as *A Stand in the Mountains*—that is, an old-fashioned Southern summer resort.

Interviewer: Now, the obligatory finale: What is the function of the artist in society?

Taylor: I think he is the ornament of society!

Oh, there is not just one role for the artist in society. He has many roles, and he has a different role as society changes—and in different societies. In medieval society it was one thing, and in the Renaissance it became another, moving far away from doing saints in stone. He can be a seer at times, and in the 18th century he was the satirist, the artist stepping back and holding up the mirror to society.

Moreover, I don't think the same kind of person is necessarily an artist or a poet in one century as another. A lot of people would disagree, but I don't think Milton would necessarily have been a poet if he had been born in the mid-19th century. Or some other poets, Auden for instance. I think what's possible for the artist in a society attracts different kinds of people. I think Jefferson would have been a scientist in another age, and I think John Randolph of Roanoke would have been a poet or a literary man in another age. But because they lived in Virginia at that time, they both had to be politicians first, or statesmen, and they were. In Virginia at that time every intellectual pursuit was for the Commonwealth. That's an example, sort of in reverse!

Interviewer: And now?

Taylor: I think the artist's role now is to resist uniformity and all the evils of industrial society and the scientific age. The arts and the sciences *are* enemies. It's the particular against the general. The artist is something *outside* society. I don't believe in a literary profession. I think that being a writer is much more the pursuit of a religion. I have a religious feeling about it. It's not a priesthood, but it's one step back.

Index

174